The Cradle, the Cross and the Empty Tomb

A Faith We Can be Proud to Proclaim

Joel Edwards

Hodder & Stoughton
LONDON SYDNEY AUCKLAND

Unless otherwise indicated, Scripture quotations are taken from the
HOLY BIBLE, NEW INTERNATIONAL VERSION.
Copyright © 1973, 1978, 1984 by International Bible Society.
First published in Great Britain 1979
Inclusive language version 1995, 1996
Used by permission of Hodder & Stoughton. All rights reserved.
'NIV' is a registered trademark of International Bible Society.
UK trademark number 1448790.

Copyright © 2000 Joel Edwards

First published in Great Britain in 2000

The right of Joel Edwards to be identified as the Author of
the Work has been asserted by him in accordance
with the Copyright, Designs and Patents Act 1988.

10 9 8 7 6 5 4 3 2 1

British Library Cataloguing in Publication Data
A record for this book is available from the British Library

ISBN 0 340 75676 4

Typeset by Avon Dataset Ltd, Bidford-on-Avon, Warks

Printed and bound in Great Britain by
The Guernsey Press Co. Ltd, Channel Isles

Hodder & Stoughton
A Division of Hodder Headline Ltd
338 Euston Road
London NW1 3BH

Contents

1
Introduction

Proud to proclaim

> It's news I'm most proud to proclaim,
> this extraordinary Message of God's
> powerful plan to rescue everyone . . .

Romans 1:16 (The Message)

How did you feel last time you slumped anonymously into your train seat, only to spot a fellow passenger openly reading their Bible in public? If you're anything like me, you'll have got that sinking feeling that maybe you too should be brave enough to brandish your faith in broad daylight.

Perhaps there and then you made a firm decision to be slightly more adventurous and travel with your rather more modest pocket New Testament or that new edition of the Bible with its front cover looking more like a thriller novel. You may have gone for the next best option and whisked out the devotional book you bought from the church bookstore some months earlier. Maybe you did what most mortals do on public transport and consoled

1

yourself by reading someone else's newspaper.

For many of us such an event can be a deeply revealing moment. It's often the point at which we are confronted with our own fears and apprehensions about the Bible, the Church and all that it means to be a Christian. It may be that what comes to the surface of our thoughts is a basic gut-feeling of lack of confidence – a deep awareness that even though we may not actually be ashamed of the gospel, we do find it a bit embarrassing to parade it in public. Such a frightening realisation may bring us into private condemnation, which is the worst kind of condemnation because there is nowhere to hide.

Most of us don't think about it but there are many good reasons to be embarrassed by the whole business of Christianity. For over a hundred and fifty years Christians have been under pressure to be more reasonable. Some very clever people regard the onward march of science as a clear indication that people have now grown up enough not to need the God of the Bible or anyone else to save them from anything beyond human ignorance. Modern rationalism has had a very intimidating effect on many of us. It has declared that, at best, God is only a shadow of his former self and, at worst, 'God is dead'. The idea that 'God is dead' is not a suggestion that his heart stopped beating at any particular time in human history. It is merely another way of saying that he never really existed in the first place and that our conscious need to think of him as existing is now redundant. In philosophical terms, 'God' has passed his sell-by date but only the smart ones know it.

If God is no longer or never was, then it only stands to reason that anything which talks about him and his unusual activities is also redundant. Miracles lose their magic – so to speak – and Christians are foolish. For if everything ultimately has a scientific explanation – including the very beginning of time – only the stubborn and unthinkingly superstitious need miracles. In this 'intelligent' scheme of things, miracles are only events awaiting an explanation. Nothing outside of our control must be allowed to exist and sooner or later we will make sense of everything.

Christianity has been beaten up in the classroom. From elaborate charts confidently explaining the origins of life on the planet, with omissions that simply pretend that God is not there, we have been educated to talk about God's activities as though he was absent from the room. The modern mind has developed a habit of talking around God as though he was severely disabled. Most explanations about unusual phenomena are gratefully received as long as they do not present God as an objective reality.

No one in their right mind devalues the benefits brought to us by reason and technology. But they didn't restrain us from slaughtering each other by the millions during two major world wars, which we will remember long into the third millennium. Nor have they done much to protect us from our dysfunctioning families and communities. No one has been able to draw a graph which proves that the more we have the happier we are. There is no scientific evidence to prove that the more we know the better we sleep at nights. So, sooner or later cracks are bound to appear on this kind of hard-surface thinking, and today there are many fingers pointing in many directions.

In fact the problem is that there are an awful lot of fingers pointing in an awful lot of very different directions. The modernity that led to the intellectual interrogation of the Church is still with us but now has to share space with a new idea. It is the non-preferential culture of our day which regards everybody and everything with equal non-respect. It's the attitude that gave Spice Girl Geri the self-appointed right to snuggle up to Prince Charles and Nelson Mandela in photo shoots. When a teenager shouts across the road to a man old enough to be his father, ''Ere, mate! Got the time?' he is drinking from the same cultural fountain. Everything has the same value, but then certain vital things can be overlooked.

So not only are Christians under threat from rampant cynicism, but also we are in danger of being ignored. And that is very embarrassing. Christians began the twenty-first century with a sobering wake-up call from the English Churches' attendance survey, 'The Tide is Running Out', which showed that church attendance had fallen from 11.5 per cent of the population to 7.5 per cent over twenty years – a loss of half a million people. Only 5 per cent of children now have any regular contact with church.

People are ignoring the Church because they now have so many other places in which to worship. You can take your pick from sports and shopping on Sundays to selecting from a range of spiritualities so wide that it's hard to tell who is walking down the right path.

It's not that people no longer believe in God. More than 70 per cent of adults do. It's just that he doesn't have to be the God of the Bible. It's fine to believe as long as 'God' makes no moral demands on us. Gods who let us get on with our lives and who stay on stand-by for the awkward patches in life are fine. People can cope with fair-weather friends and bad weather gods. Any god who comes crashing in to make demands on our sex lives and on what we do with our money or who expects us to be inconvenienced in any way is not normally very welcome, but too often that is the impression Christians have given about God. The last thing we want is to sound like unthinking bigots, full of convictions and light on brains. Christianity can seem like that with talk about sin, heaven and hell. Talk of a God who makes demands and threatens people with eternal damnation if they fail to co-operate can be hard to handle at a funeral service. It is difficult to say that God claims to love everyone but lets bad things happen, because that does not sound much like good news to most people in the real world. It can leave Christians struggling embarrassingly to find good explanations in crises.

Sings out of season

I was travelling to work on the London Underground. As we came into a station, the usual mechanical voice said, 'This is

Holborn. Change here for the Piccadilly line.' I looked up from my book and, sure enough, it was Holborn. The doors opened; the message was repeated. The doors closed; and we heard the same information. We rumbled out of the station and into the darkness, but again the voice said, 'This is Holborn. Change here for the Piccadilly line.' The helpful voice had become as dated as Christmas carols in July.

Just when Christians were getting to grips with the 'scientific' proofs that the Bible is as reliable as any other book, full of factual history and supported by archaeological findings, people are losing interest in facts and going in for feelings in a big way. The Church talks about what is true and most of our friends are more interested in what is real for them. It's as though Christians are out of kilter, answering questions no one outside is asking and offering opinions which seem out of date. And who wants to feel dated when novelty is all the rage?

Credibility count

In 1998 the Henley Centre conducted a survey, 'Planning for Social Change' to establish which brand names the general public really trusted. The Church and its leaders came after eight other brands, one of which was Kellogg's. People said they could tell what was in the Kellogg's box by reading the label but they couldn't be so sure about the Church.

The survey was not unlike the one conducted by *The Sunday Times* on 7 February 1999, asking people in Britain to identify the nation's spiritual leader. Prime Minister Tony Blair was identified as the number one choice among adults and Sir Bobby Charlton, the football player who formed part of the squad who won the 1966 World Cup, was identified as the spiritual leader for youngsters under sixteen.

Christianity has a credibility problem. Christians are not taken seriously, for a number of good reasons. Newspapers provide a constant stream of sensational bad news about church people who abuse children or commit other misdemeanours. It certainly does not help matters to have senior church leaders who challenge historically orthodox teachings. Headlines such as 'Third of clergy do not believe in Virgin Birth' and 'Today's priests "embarrassed to talk of Hell"' (*The Times*, 17 July 1999) only add to a growing atmosphere of doubt, which undermines the confidence of Christians as we try to talk to others about God.

To make things worse, Christians are easy targets on TV. Soap operas such as *EastEnders* seem to enjoy portraying unhelpful caricatures of Christians who fit comfortably in the 'weirdos for Jesus' pigeonhole. Unfortunately, these characters are not entirely fictitious. Most churches have at least one.

The Bible and the bullet

The late Lesslie Newbigin once wrote, 'The sins which deface the Church do not destroy the power of the gospel.' We all say, 'Amen!' The only problem is that the people we are trying to convince often don't see it that way. They are easily distracted by unsavoury elements of church history. Indeed, Melvyn Bragg's twenty-week series, *Two Thousand Years*, celebrating the history of Christianity in the build-up to the millennium, had as much focus on these issues as it did on the triumphs of the Christian Church.

People remember the Spanish Inquisition and the cruelties of the Crusades which led to the deaths of thousands of Jews and Muslims. Black activists reflect on the Church's involvement in slavery and the collaboration between the bullet and the Bible in the missionary enterprise of the eighteenth and nineteenth centuries. They remember South African apartheid and America's Ku Klux Klan. Instead of 'peace on earth', our neighbours are often stuck with images of Northern Ireland and confusing notions of Catholics and Protestants fighting over old scores.

Women have had an age-old argument with the Church, seeing it as a major agent of repression and the province of male dominance. The rise of feminist theology has been one important protest against this repressive view of the Church.

As a small girl, my daughter used to be very reluctant to answer the phone. She used to think that she wouldn't know what to say. It's probably close to the feeling which most Christians get when the Jehovah's Witness knocks at the door on a Saturday morning, armed with literature, small children and a persistent smile. Most of us make excuses about being busy. We tend to say it's a 'bad time', although we are usually pushed to say when a 'good time' might be. The truth of the matter is that many Christians fear the ensuing doorstep discussion would show up their own ignorance about their faith. Even if we know *what* we believe, we are not always sure *why* we believe it.

Despite the fact that we have around twenty main English versions of the Bible, up to 66 per cent of regular churchgoers in the UK do not read it from one week to the next. The average Christian is usually woefully aware of the bareness of their biblical knowledge.

What miracle?

The greatest credibility gap is that between what we read in the Bible and what happens in our own experience. It is one thing to read about the miracles of Jesus and to sing that 'he is the same today', but most of us go for years without seeing a miracle beyond the wonder of our conversion experience. If the truth be told, what often gets marked up as a miracle sometimes leaves us wondering whether the pills triumphed over prayers. We don't have many Lazaruses sitting along the row from us on Sunday mornings.

Within charismatic churches all over the world there is a steady flow of disillusioned believers who are struggling with prophetic promises which missed the mark by miles. Frankly, if half of the prophetic 'words' uttered on Sundays across the world were true the world would be a noticeably better place. But my point is not to be anti-prophetic, because I owe a great deal to accurate and affirming prophecies that have deeply influenced my life. My purpose here is merely to draw attention to the fact that there are attempts to speak on God's behalf that have backfired in too many lives.

And it gets worse. Many of us read, sing and talk about 'victory' without knowing what it means. Only we ourselves know the suffocating cell of disaffection in which we feel trapped when the things we have long prayed for do not arrive. In this place of disaffection, resentment often lives next door. It can be hard to talk of 'victory' from such a place.

People are growing tired of words – and intuitively we know it. It is little wonder that television adverts and giant billposters have become strong on images and less dependent on text. The prevalent culture is one of pragmatism, where people *may* pay attention if what we say actually *works*. Great themes and doctrines are OK if you believe them, but people look for *signs* of faith as a gateway to *ideas* about faith.

It is exceedingly hard to share our faith with others when we are struggling to grasp some of the ideas ourselves.

Preach it, Paul!

You don't have to be a scholar to know that the apostle Paul was a very unusual person. He had an irrepressible spirit which shines through much of what he wrote. There are many things about Paul with which we can readily identify. The 'thorn in his flesh' (2 Corinthians 12:7), his weakness and shaking knees (1 Corinthians 2:3) are all clear indications that, whatever else he was, he was certainly one of us.

But it's his certainty and confidence which begins to distance us from him. And this is exemplified in his attitude to the gospel. There is no sense of diffidence or procrastination in his proclamation of the good news about Jesus. Yet Paul, the scholarly, ex-orthodox Jew, had been a murderer and persecutor of Christians, who undoubtedly had to beg forgiveness for years after his conversion as he continued to run into Christian Jews whose relatives he had conspired to kill. Paul – the imperfect perfectionist who wanted to find out the true reasons for his own conversion (Philippians 3:12) – was a man passionate to preach.

Of all places, Paul was anxious to proclaim the gospel in Rome, the epicentre of the known world. It was associated with prestige, culture and political power. From here the emperor dominated the world by his own self-appointed deity and military strength, but it was also a desperate place. In the great arenas, human lives were spent in the pursuit of pleasure. Sexual perversion had already sowed the seeds of Rome's destruction; corruption and political paranoia were rampant. And Rome was restless with the new sect called 'Christians'. Rome was a tough place to be a Christian, but Paul was not put off. He was not ashamed of the gospel and he wanted to preach it in Rome (Romans 1:15–16).

So just why was Paul so unashamedly keen to take the gospel to Rome? Certainly this was not Paul, the new convert, wet behind the ears and still a little naive. Paul had collected enough unhappy stories about church life, in fights and problems with opposition, to last him a lifetime. By this stage he is a seasoned Christian and his eagerness to go to Rome is recorded in one of the most mature and theological books of the New Testament. His grasp of the good news must have given him some confidence. As a Roman citizen he would also have had some confidence in his ability to work cross-culturally in the Roman context. In fact, his knowledge of Rome must have prepared him for the level of cynicism and disbelief he was guaranteed to attract in the self-sufficient confidence of Rome. But the real source of his confidence lay elsewhere. Paul well understood that his strength lay not in human wisdom but in God's power. As he explained to the Christians in Corinth:

When I came to you, brothers and sisters, I did not come with eloquence or superior wisdom as I proclaimed to you the testimony about God. For I resolved to know nothing while I was with you except Jesus Christ and him crucified. I came to you in weakness and fear, and with much trembling. My message and my preaching were not with wise and persuasive words, but with a demonstration of the Spirit's power, so that your faith might not rest on human wisdom, but on God's power.

1 Corinthians 2:1–5

Paul was only too aware that for many people in Corinth, as in Rome, his testimony was 'foolishness', but he was prepared to risk it. If you are to proclaim something, there is no way around the risk involved.

But Paul could not get away from another important reality. The gospel actually works! He simply could not deny the radical change that had taken place in his life. The power of the gospel rested in the application of faith. Like so many others around him he had stumbled on an old truth, 'The righteous will live by faith' (Romans 1:17).

Paul was not ashamed because he never lost sight of what the gospel was all about. It was not about church politics, neither did it depend on his own ability to articulate its complex ideas. Paul knew that the gospel, quite simply, is the durable story of how God sent Jesus to be born on earth, to live a life among us, then to die for our sins, and to be raised from death. Paul did more than anyone else to help us make sense of these strange notions. He knew too that all of us would struggle to fully understand the enormity of these claims.

But just like the other apostles of his day he kept talking about three things: the fact that Jesus Christ was born as a human baby, the fact that he died a real death, and the fact that he rose bodily from death. These three irresistible snapshots form the basis of the good news. Again and again the young Church held up the symbols of the baby, the cross and the discarded tomb. It seemed to resonate with the experiences and the needs of the people around them. It took the Church another four hundred years to work out more of the details behind these symbols, but as they proclaimed the cradle, the cross and the empty tomb of Jesus, they found their world was changing around them.

As Paul wrote, 'It's news I'm most proud to proclaim, this extraordinary Message of God's powerful plan to rescue everyone' (Romans 1:16, *The Message*), we too can be proud to proclaim the Jesus of the cradle, the cross and empty tomb.

The Cradle

For unto us a child is born,
unto us a son is given . . .

Isaiah 9:6 (AV)

Small Christmas gifts handed over with the announcement that 'good things come in small parcels' can create suspicion. It is the perfect thing to say if you want a cover for being mean. But sometimes it is true. You don't need a double-decker bus to deliver a diamond ring.

The story of Jesus in a manger is meant to be for life – not just for Christmas. It is the story of God accommodating himself to us. But it is far more than that; it is a symbol of his total identification with anyone who feels vulnerable.

PART ONE

The Cradle

Adventure is a child's born,
life is a gift given.

James 4:14 NIV

2
God: The Baby in an Ox's Stall

In a most unlikely place, an angel crept up on a young woman to make a grand announcement. The young woman was probably a teenager. The angel came to say that God had a plan and that he, Gabriel, had arrived hot-winged to tell her about it. The plan was rather ambitious. In fact, it was God's biggest idea yet.

It was, quite simply, to save the world. God's most urgent concern was the fact that people – all types of people all over the world – needed forgiveness. But the plan was as complex as it was ambitious. Not only was he to provide the means of salvation, but also he himself was to *be* the means of that salvation. The really amazing thing was that he would do it by making the young woman have a baby. The normal process was to be short-circuited; the Holy Spirit would come close enough to her to accomplish this incredible thing so that the child, strictly speaking, would be nothing to do with the woman's fiancé.

Mary was left alone with her head spinning. In those brief, breathless moments, her future rolled out before her. She knew the problems this would cause in her own family and the embarrassment for her betrothed, Joseph, and his relatives; the explanations that wouldn't add up; the disbelief and whisperings around Nazareth where everybody knew everybody else's business. She had no way of knowing yet about the horrible journey she would need to make, travelling eighty miles south, uphill to Bethlehem, on a donkey's back when she was heavily pregnant.

Mary was shell-shocked and couldn't believe it at first. Her recollection of those first few moments with the angel and her incredulity at his message must for all time have given her a sympathetic hearing from anyone who wrestled with her amazing story. But it is little wonder that after her magnificent outburst (Luke 1:46–55) she fell into an almost complete silence for the rest of the New Testament.

The thought of a new start in a new place may have been an incentive to take the long journey to Bethlehem from Nazareth. In Bethlehem people might make kinder assumptions about Mary and Joseph, who wouldn't have to give the real version of events if they really didn't want to. But it must have been a short-lived pipe dream. To return to your 'home town' as total strangers couldn't have been much fun, and door-knocking for a spare room only to end up in a manger, for a mother-to-be, must have been an ordeal.

Just when they thought they were safe from rumours, a gentle flow of distant relatives began to appear. Members of Joseph's extended family also returned to Bethlehem. They had come to bring Caesar's poll tax, but they also brought searching questions, which Mary and Joseph stuttered to answer.

Then came the inevitable day when the crushing contractions came, shaking the young girl as she lay on the stable floor. The overpowering and inescapable feelings of acute discomfort, much worse than those of being caught with a full bladder in an inconvenient place. The rushing water, the flush of a raised temperature and the sharp pains of birth. Her body buckled to deliver the Promise. The blood and the protruding head. The urgent, complaining cry of a brand-new baby. And who knew? Was she alone with Joseph, or may we safely assume that his parents were there to help? Did strangers rush to her aid as Joseph paced the open field outside the stable door, or was he the bewildered midwife?

Before she knew it, Mary's wrinkled baby was the centre of attention. The unexpected visits of the shepherds and the wise men must have been both flattering and overwhelming in equal measure. But it would have been all too much for the young couple. Between the nappy changes and breast-feeding, Mary's thoughts raced ahead, anticipating what the angel could possibly have meant about her son's future. It wasn't long before word had gone out that the small bundle of life in Joseph's arms was some sort of threat to Herod, the puppet king. Inevitably, Herod began looking for the baby. Eventually, under the cloak of night, Joseph and Mary packed everything they had and crept out of Bethlehem. They headed out for an unknown destination to become refugees in Egypt. It would have been hard enough to bring up this unusual child, but to do so under such strange and demanding circumstances must have taken a great deal of courage.

In spite of what parents read in books about parenting, most of us end up improvising along the way. There are some things one simply cannot be prepared for. Mary's experience would have taken her a lifetime to unravel. Indeed, one gets the impression that she never fully understood her eldest son. She was amazed to discover Jesus engrossed in conversation with members of the intellectual elite at the age of twelve, appeared tentatively in the background throughout his ministry and was beside herself with grief at his crucifixion. If Mary found it hard to make sense of events to which she was so closely related, it is hardly surprising that many of us since then have struggled to get our minds around the concept of God as a baby, with a feeding trough for animals as his cradle.

'Can we believe the Christmas story?' was the title that Channel 4 gave to a television discussion in which I was one of three panellists in 1997. My colleagues on that occasion were an Anglican priest, Donald Reeves, and an academic, Peter Atkins. Donald insisted that he wasn't a liberal Christian, but he refused to say whether he thought Mary was a virgin. Peter described himself as an enthusiastic atheist whose mission in life was to discredit faith. Much of the discussion centred around questions about the historical reliability of the biblical accounts of the nativity. At its heart, the debate was questioning who Jesus really was. Even when we defend the historicity of the gospel narratives about Jesus's birth, we know that there is something behind and beyond the factual accounts of his birth which doesn't quite 'add up'. How can any one person be truly God and completely human?

When Gabriel told her she was about to have a baby, Mary's natural question had been, 'How will this be . . . since I am a virgin?' In brief, Gabriel's explanation was that nothing was too hard for God. There is little to indicate that Mary had any understanding of the details of the mechanics behind this great mystery. It must have been hard for Mary to take in what Gabriel said to her. The Bible never presents her as a great teacher of mysteries but almost always as a mysterious figure. Throughout Jesus's growing years and adult life – right up to the point of his death and resurrection, and even in the upper room on the Day of Pentecost – Mary is presented as her son's disciple, loyally present, always waiting to learn more. Throughout the New Testament she is depicted as a woman quietly trying to understand, one who 'treasured up . . . and pondered . . . in her heart' things about Jesus (Luke 2:19).

She wasn't to be the only one. It took the Church over four hundred years to agree upon a set of words which remotely made sense of the mystery of the incarnation. The great Council of

Nicea in AD 325 produced the Church's best response to Mary's original question to Gabriel.

> For us and for our salvation
> He came down from heaven,
> Was incarnate of the Holy Spirit and the Virgin Mary
> And became truly human.
> For our sake he was crucified under Pontius Pilate;
> He suffered death and was buried.
> On the third day he rose again
> In accordance with the Holy Scriptures.

In the closing stages of the twentieth century, the General Synod of the Church of England was locked in earnest debate. The House of Bishops, having decided upon a subtle but important change to the ancient Nicene Creed, brought it to the Synod for agreement. There a prominent Archdeacon, the Venerable Pete Broadbent, challenged them to think again. The debate concerned a small Greek word, *ek*. The preposition could be translated in different ways, either making Mary a co-equal of the Holy Spirit in Jesus's birth or putting her in a subordinate role. The House of Bishops was happy to make her co-equal; the Venerable Broadbent and other members of Synod strongly disagreed. It was Mary's question all over again. Finally in March 2000, the Synod voted to include new wording in the modern-language version of the Nicene Creed: 'from the Holy Spirit and the Virgin Mary', with effect from 1 December 2000.

Such debates are important but they also show us just how difficult the subject of the incarnation has always been. Today, belief in the virgin birth is losing ground. 'Modern Believing', a survey conducted in July 1999 to trace trends in Christian doctrine since 1960, showed that only half those questioned still believe it is true. Within the Free Churches, only 28 per cent of respondents took it literally. In 1996 only a worrying 69 per cent of Free

Church full-time clergy and 82 per cent of retired clergy had said the virgin birth was factual.

But the vast majority of Christians do believe in the virgin birth. And with good reasons. For one thing, this is the claim of Scripture (Isaiah 7:14; Matthew 1:18–25; Luke 1:26–38). Admittedly, 'virgin' strictly refers to a young woman but the biblical implication is clear. A careful look at the Gospels reveals an important piece of chronology. It is evident that Elizabeth, Mary's elderly relative, became aware that she was due to have a baby before Mary did (Luke 1:23–6). Once Mary received her news from the angel Gabriel, it seems clear that she set off very soon to visit Elizabeth (Luke 1:39). She then stayed with Elizabeth for three months (Luke 1:56), presumably returning to her home in Nazareth just before the birth of John the Baptist. What is important here is that we are left with the very firm impression that Mary was nowhere near Joseph for at least the first three months of her pregnancy. We don't know exactly when Mary and Joseph were married but it isn't unreasonable to assume that it was between three to five months into her pregnancy. This means that Luke certainly took the virgin birth seriously.

Credible Christianity defends the virgin birth. It is the only way to make sense of the story of Jesus's birth and sinless life. If there are doubts about it, these arise not because the idea is inconsistent with the stories of his death and resurrection but because of difficulties with believing in a God who does miracles. This is the reason why those who dismiss the virgin birth generally dismiss the historical reality of Jesus's death and resurrection too. But this is also precisely why believers take them all to be elements of the same story.

So it is surprising, perhaps, that outside the Gospels, the rest of the New Testament appears to be rather indifferent to any historical claim for the virgin birth of Jesus. None of the apostles mentioned it in their early preaching and Paul totally ignored it in his writings. In fact it seems that the virgin birth was never presented as a proof that Jesus was really the Son of God in the same way that his death and resurrection were (see, for example, Romans 1:3–4). Frankly, the virgin birth – important though it is to us – has less provable weight. It is relatively easy to write it off as a personal matter between Mary and Joseph, a private fantasy concocted to hide their embarrassment.

It is even more likely that Mary and Joseph said little about the virgin birth. The price of claiming to be the one who brought God into the world would have been very high. Better to leave room for speculation and embarrassment. And embarrassing it would have been! Assuming that Mary was still in her parents' home in the very early stages of her pregnancy, she would have had some explaining to do. What on earth would she say about the morning sickness? We may well imagine that Mary was locked into a suffocating cell of secrecy. It all makes better sense of her meeting with her older relative, Elizabeth. It was no accident that Mary was so keen to see her after the angel said, 'Even Elizabeth your relative is going to have a child in her old age' (Luke 1:36). We all know how soothing it can be to find someone else in a similar predicament when explanations run dry. The very fact that Elizabeth's six-month pregnancy had to be announced to Mary by an angel shows just how much of a secret it had been. But it was more than that. Elizabeth, more than anyone else, would understand the inexplicable. Those three months with Elizabeth and Zechariah would have been a tonic to the young girl. When the two women met, there were no other mothers like them in the whole world and they knew it. Their meeting was an overflow of joy and prophetic insights, but it was also likely to have been sheer relief for Mary.

The fact that we cannot adequately explain the details of the virgin birth isn't a good reason for dismissing it. In fact, any who regard themselves as thinking persons should have an intellectual struggle with the virgin birth. If Mary had had the capacity to understand this mystery, her attitude throughout the New

Testament would have been very different. The very fact that she was pressed into silence and awe by the wonder of it all is in itself a signal for the rest of us. And if such a great crowd of Christian witnesses can scarcely make rational sense of it, we shouldn't be surprised that many of our friends won't either.

But perhaps that is the problem for us. To describe a mystery is no mean feat. And this is often one of our greatest difficulties in seeking to present the gospel without being embarrassed. We feel like a salesman floundering on the doorstep, having left the training course halfway through. We are confident to talk as long as the potential customer doesn't have any questions about the product. But people have a lot of questions to ask. Academics may have a smart response to offer, but most of us will be lost for words – unless we can give meaning to the mystery. So, like Mary, Christians are caught in the middle. We cannot fully explain the virgin birth, but we have come to know it is true.

In reality, God could have made Jesus entirely holy by hijacking the humanity of a teenage Jesus and infusing him with holiness. He could have chosen a thirty-year-old man, emptied him of sin and presented the world with an adopted Messiah. But God wanted to do something greater. He wanted to show his willingness to be vulnerable.

When my wife was six months' pregnant with our daughter, she slipped down the stairs, injuring her coccyx. From that moment on, we harboured a faint concern about the rest of the pregnancy. Most of us know just how cautious we are likely to be around pregnant women. Fathers-to-be can be a real bore! The reason is simple: we are all aware of the potential for life and also the fragility of a woman's womb at such a time. Joseph would have been no different. In fact, my guess is that he was more cautious than the average expectant father.

Jesus was vulnerable in Mary's womb. What might have happened had she slipped on a piece of Jaffa orange peel seven months into her pregnancy? God trusted Mary and Joseph to protect the baby in Mary's womb. To nourish and care for the newborn infant. To do the nappy changes and avoid nappy rashes. To guard his life from Herod's threats even when it meant rushing away as refugees to Egypt. And when the rumours of Herod's genocide finally reached Mary and Joseph from the safety of Egypt, it must have added to their pain that their safety cost so many lives. Was one speechless infant really worth so many?

Mary's merry Christmas

Mary was probably excited but not all that merry on that first Christmas. She had a lot to worry about. Apart from the thrill of having her first baby, there was very little in it for her as far as she could tell. The wrinkled bundle of humanity was only a promise of things she couldn't fully understand. This was a complex experience and in her mind she wondered about the paradox of the thrill of the promise and the arduous reality and problems. She would have little affinity with our sanitised Christmas-card versions of the nativity, which distance themselves from any notion of pain.

This is the abiding power of the cradle of Christ. This is why we needn't be ashamed. Gabriel's earlier announcement to Mary said it in a soundbite: Emmanuel – 'God with us'. No one can take the Christmas story seriously and fail to see the point. Even if the story is reduced to a myth it is still difficult to avoid the big idea. The Christmas event is God's advertising campaign telling us that he is often at his best when we are in difficult situations.

As an integral part of a one-hour, Christmas Day *Gospel Special* service at which I was the speaker, broadcast by the BBC in 1999, we heard the story of the Doyley family. I had known the Doyleys for a number of years and it was very moving to hear how Christmas had come to be a bittersweet time for them, following the death of the father of the family two Christmases earlier. Their contribution to the service included a Bob Marley composition sung by five brothers in memory of their father, and personal accounts from his wife and daughter. What came across very clearly was the sadness and even the sense of betrayal they all felt when the father died shortly before Christmas, but also the reassurance they had that God was still with them. I suggested to the producer that she was walking an emotional tightrope by including such a tear-jerker in a Christmas Day service. She felt, quite rightly, that it would resonate with many viewers who would be watching from the solitude of their homes, with their own mixed memories.

Mary would have been at home in the pain of the Doyleys' Christmas as they sat around wondering why their father had died. And in the same way she would have slotted into the many homes for which Christmas is one of the most stressful times of the year. The problem is that for many Christians, Christmas has become a sanitised experience. Most of us have drifted away from the authentic Christmas event because we have been sheltered by lifestyles and safe church-based events which bear no resemblance to the extraordinariness of Mary's first Christmas, or the bitter weeping of the mothers who lost their babies as a result of Herod's insecurity. But the message is clear: God begins with vulnerability.

Some years ago while I was a pastor, Paulette, a church member and an ambulance driver, shocked me with a matter-of-fact piece of information. In a casual conversation just before one Christmas period, I suggested that she would probably have a fairly easy time over the holiday. 'Oh, no!' she said with a tolerant chuckle. 'Christmas is the busiest time of the year!' I found out later on that, amid the unparalleled shopping and festivities, over 750,000 people in Britain are caught up in domestic arguments every Christmas. The police usually describe 50 per cent of these incidents as 'serious'. In fact Christmas shows up on Holmes and Rahe's 'Social Adjustment Rating Scale' (1967) as one of the most stressful experiences people have. Admittedly it is second from last, but it is worth bearing in mind that the season of joy, peace and goodwill to all humankind turns up on the same emotional

Richter-scale as death, divorce and trouble with the boss. There are a lot of people for whom December to January each year may be regarded as the 'stressmass' season.

Even if it is boring, we mustn't fail to remind people that the baby in the cradle didn't come to offer peace only in the absence of our problems. The gospel for our modern world offers peace without pretence. It doesn't pretend that all is well when that isn't the case. This is the way we make sense of Jesus's cradle to a world that is wide-eyed for explanations. The baby in the manger is an unmistakable token of God's deep interest in the full range of human life.

From the cradle to the grave – and beyond

In an address to the Baptist Union of Scotland in 1998, Douglas McBain reminded his hearers that when a society goes off the rails the first to suffer are usually the children. His reference was to child sacrifice during a low point in Israel's history, but the principle still holds true today, as can be seen from the numbers of abortions being carried out, and the rising statistics of cases of child abuse.

No one pretends that the issue of abortion is simple. It is singularly unhelpful when Christian ethics on this matter present it in a dismissive, matter-of-fact way. There is more than principle involved; every discussion about the life of an unborn infant is also a discussion about the future of its parents. And as we all know, the discussions about when life actually begins will always be a point of controversy between pro- and anti-abortionists.

Britain ended the twentieth century with an appalling account of over six million aborted foetuses since the Abortion Act was introduced in 1967. Few Christians in Britain want to be associated with the more extreme behaviour of 'moral majority' evangelicalism in the United States, but we have a right to share its passion and outrage at the killing of millions of vulnerable children in the womb. The situation has become even more disturbing with reports of a growing industry in the sale of 'spare parts' from aborted babies in the USA and Britain.

Abortion has been and will continue to be a contentious issue in the twenty-first century. Angular crusader attitudes toward abortionists are unlikely to win the day, and all the evidence is that they haven't taken us very far over the last thirty years. As Christians we must come to the debate with firm convictions but also with empathy and a willingness to understand that others simply don't share our world-view or values. Personally, I am equally concerned about Christian mission that focuses on abortion to the exclusion of everything else. It is unbiblical to lobby Parliament on abortion while despising the poor or the prisoner. In fact the Bible is far more explicit about these causes (Matthew 25:31–46).

A Christian approach to abortion doesn't imply a laissez-faire attitude to one of society's greatest scourges. The sad truth is that we are making little impact in reversing the trend towards abortion on demand. Despite sustained professionalism and focused energy from committed pro-life agencies, both Christian and non-Christian, society has sold out to a quick-fix mentality. The easiest thing for the Christian community to do in the years ahead will be to abandon the cause, to go with the flow and campaign on other issues in which success may appear more easily come by.

But good news cannot walk away from unborn babies who die in the womb. God became a baby and the Emmanuel event is profoundly concerned about it. Creation speaks clearly to us about the value of life but we must also listen to Mary's account. The cradle cries out to the people of the twenty-first century to think again. Throughout the Bible God honoured the process of birth. Mary's womb was blessed and Christmas is a reminder that he is pleased to be implicated in the most vulnerable stages of human existence.

Emmanuel doesn't abandon us at birth. It is therefore impossible to separate the good news of the gospel from the plight of many young children across the world who are at risk from adults. The twenty-first century isn't likely to see an end to the growing numbers of vulnerable children. It is an irony of our times that we are increasingly prone to crush the defenceless while we believe we are growing more sophisticated as a civilisation. Across the world children are increasingly becoming the sexual chattels of perverted adults.

Most of us were taken by storm when the NSPCC published its report in March 1999 showing a rising tide of domestic child abuse. *The Times* (16 March) ran the headline: 'At home and so at risk: Cruelty to children demands state intervention in the family – and fast'. The report showed that a quarter of all rape victims are children, that 100 children a year are being killed and that new babies were five times more likely to be killed than adults. In the same year, 35,000 children were on the child protection register.

The gospel has something to say to them, and to the street children in Latin America, South Africa and elsewhere. Only a person who has ignored the history of the Church in the eighteenth and nineteenth centuries will fail to see the extent to which good news, through missionaries who sacrificed themselves for children at risk, reached into the streets to care for and educate children across the world. The very same compulsion to care drove reformers to emancipate children from the mines and factories in Dickensian Britain and trained countless Sunday school students throughout the Western world.

The Church has been guilty of abuse but it has also been involved in the care of those at risk, as an integral part of its mission. This hasn't always been prompted by 'do-gooders'. In the main it has been because Christians are inspired by the belief that God is on the side of the vulnerable. It is a claim of the incarnation about which we needn't be ashamed.

Women

Hamlet wasn't pleased with his mother, Gertrude, the queen. A memorable line from the play has stayed with me over the years. 'Frailty, thy name is woman!' Hamlet ranted, in despair at his mother's precipitate marriage to her husband's brother, who was also his murderer. Later in the play Hamlet rejected Ophelia, with whom he had been in love, encouraging her to go off to a nunnery. This isn't exactly behaviour designed to impress a twenty-first-century woman, but it wouldn't have been all that uncommon an attitude in first-century Israel. An orthodox Jewish prayer ran, 'I thank you, God, that I was born neither a woman nor a Gentile dog'!

In a culture where women and children were often treated as second-class citizens without political or domestic franchise, they were among the vulnerable dispossessed. It has to be said that this wasn't unique to the Jews. In first-century cultures generally, women had few privileges to speak of. But it was into this very environment that the God-man came. Paul's record in the letter to the Christians in Galatia is interesting: 'But when the time had fully come, God sent his Son, born of a woman, born under law, to redeem those under law, that we might receive adoption as God's children' (Galatians 4:4).

I once saw a cartoon in a Christian publication which had me smiling for ages. It was a drawing of St Paul arriving at Corinth by boat. The quay is packed with angry women waving hostile placards saying things like, 'Down with Paul!' 'Paul is a woman-hater!' 'Go home, Paul!' and 'Paul is a chauvinist pig!' Paul, however, is smiling benignly and says, 'Ah! I see you got my letter, then!'

I believe Paul has had a rough press as an anti-feminist. To regard Paul as a misogynist is a gross misrepresentation of the man. He was certainly a child of his times and would therefore have written and preached within the context of his dual culture as a Jewish scholar and a Roman citizen. Much of what he had to say about the role of women in the worship setting and teaching ministry, as in his letters to the Christians in Corinth, was expressed within the context of his time. To read him through the lenses of post-feminist culture isn't particularly helpful. He was, to say the least, ambiguous on many issues we now struggle with today. Even Peter admitted, 'His letters contain some things that are hard to understand' (2 Peter 3:16). But to write him off as an unqualified woman-hater is to read him inappropriately. Worse still, it is to miss the extent to which Paul's ministry sowed the seeds of subversion under the topsoil of his culture.

My purpose here isn't to open out the complex and much-rehearsed discussions about the role of women in leadership, the Church or society. But it is to draw us back to the point of vulnerability. In Galatians 4:4, Paul is quite keen to state the obvious. God used a *woman* to bring the Messiah. Biologically it could have been no other way. But in terms of its significance for women God would *have* it no other way. From the very beginning the promise was that a virgin would have a son (Isaiah 9:6).

Luke's Gospel uncompromisingly positions Elizabeth and Mary on centre stage, along with Zechariah, in the opening scenes of the great drama. 'Highly favoured' women (Luke 1:28) come few and far between in any culture. But teenager Mary was distinctive. Her dependent bundle of life in the cradle made all the difference. As far as Luke the Gentile doctor was concerned, God had turned a new page in history. So Luke began as he meant to continue, highlighting women in the life of Jesus. He refers to thirteen women, such as the widow of Nain (Luke 7:11–17) for example, not mentioned in any other Gospel. In Luke, women are particularly prominent at Jesus's crucifixion and resurrection.

Paul is consistent with Luke even though he is working not just with the story of Jesus's life and death, but with its implications for the Church and all human life. However imperfectly he does it, Paul, more than any other New Testament writer, attempted to draw out the implications of the incarnation for vulnerable women in the first century AD.

No woman in Paul's day would have been shocked to hear that she should submit to her husband (Ephesians 5:22). He may just as well have said, 'The sky will be blue if the clouds get out of the way.' Culturally, it was a non-statement. If you owned nothing, had no right to trade without your husband's consent and could be divorced at the drop of your husband's hat, it was rather easy to submit. But Paul's idea that husbands were to love their wives as they loved themselves would have been quite radical in the first-century community. It is unlikely that bigoted first-century men would take kindly to having a single man tell them to love their wives with that kind of commitment. Paul was equally unconventional in advocating mutuality in sexual relationships within marriage by suggesting that each partner had equal access to the other's body (1 Corinthians 7:3–4). The men at Ephesus and Corinth may well have been tempted to form a 'reception committee' similar to the one in Corinth I mentioned earlier!

Christians have often been confused or hesitant, or encountered difficulties about the role of women, who for far too long have been at the bottom of the vulnerability pile in Church and society. The Church has been guilty of oppressing and repressing women. Legitimate arguments about leadership have led not only to the absence of women from public platforms, but also on occasions to a quiet and unintentional suffocation of God-given ministries in the body of Christ. The Church has also played its role in the conspiracy to subdue women in the wider society.

Like it or not, we owe a debt to aspects of feminism which have pushed us all to think again about what it really means to believe that men and women are made in God's image and likeness. As a result, many of us have seriously reviewed our understanding of the 'priesthood of *all* believers'.

I was surprised to learn recently that, in spite of the progress of the women's movement over the past hundred years, clinical experience has shown that women in the West are becoming *more* insecure. With the rise of the Western professional woman, a strange irony still exists in our society of 'successful' women who are not coping. The dilemma has been popularised by American soap operas such as *Friends*, and *Ally McBeal*, in which an attractive thirty-something lawyer struggles to find a satisfactory relationship. Women are still more likely to suffer from anxiety, trauma and nervous tensions. More women are now being incarcerated than ever before. In other parts of the world women continue to bear the brunt of society's maladies. The fact that a few women have emerged as world leaders in Europe and the East does little to offset that fact.

Luke and Paul are on the same side. The gospel of Jesus brought with it a new dignity for the masses of women who would otherwise have no sense of value. Even where the Church has failed to live up to its mandate in this respect, the challenge of the gospel is to be true to what God intended by sending his Spirit on his 'sons *and* daughters' (Acts 2:17). In the gospel there is a message of hope which doesn't exclude women.

What is clear is that those who gathered around the stable after the birth of Jesus ranged from the privileged Eastern 'wise men' – who took enormous risks with their own reputation and safety in betraying Herod – to the humble shepherds. Actually, the truth of the matter is that shepherds weren't necessarily humble. They were certainly at the bottom end of the social pile. Many of them, though, were probably very untrustworthy. If you were a shepherd, not only was it a dead-end job; it also meant that you belonged to a trade with zero status and your word would usually count for nothing in a court of law. If you were a shepherd, you were definitely among the socially excluded.

Today's culture tries to hold two things in tension. First, it glorifies individualism: local histories and dialects are now more important than ever. Even the BBC doesn't mind! No one wants to be thought of as a number in the system. We struggle with any attempts to suppress our individuality. This has become a society of non-deferential treatment where everyone has equal status and equal say. These attitudes have even been woven into the fabric of our political systems with prime ministers and presidents presenting themselves casually on first-name terms.

But we are equally aware that we are all a part of an international community that is more closely networked through our technological, trading and banking systems than ever before. The speed and extent of havoc wreaked by viruses transmitted in e-mails is proof of this. The links will multiply as corporate mergers become even more popular in the twenty-first century. None of us can resist the fact that we are a part of a shrinking village through our information technology.

Some years ago I was returning from the south coast late at night. As I rushed along a dual carriageway, flashing blue lights behind me made me aware that I was in trouble. The car came up alongside my vehicle and gave me the obligatory 'pull over' signal. A policeman emerged to ask me that rhetorical question they are so good at asking, 'Do you know why I am stopping you?' Actually it was quite obvious – I was driving the second of three vehicles returning together from a very long weekend spent recording in Eastbourne and we all wanted to get home as fast as possible. Without asking me, the police officer then told me something else I knew: my name and address! In fact he politely asked me to pass on a message to the driver in the Triumph Sprint TR7 in front of me whose name and address he also knew well! It was the first time that I realised just how available technology has made all our personal details.

We must all live with the tension between how we maximise our anonymity and how well we can be known in the modern world. None of us wants to be alone and no one wants to be lost in the crowds. Something very deep within all of us refuses to be anything less than an individual. Whoever we are and wherever we come from, we refuse to be marginalised.

Something dramatic took place around the birth of Jesus, which shifted the perception of those people who were willing to pay attention to what God was doing. Around the cradle God was forming a level playing field for all who were vulnerable and marginalised. Jewish minds were forced to recognise that all classes and cultures were equally important to God as a result of the Emmanuel event (Colossians 3:11). In God's new arrangements there would be a place for all vulnerable people and it didn't matter whether they were wise men risking Herod's wrath or anonymous shepherds without status on the hills overlooking Bethlehem.

3
The God of Small Beginnings

Some men feel very uncomfortable if they have to deal with newborn babies, which seem so small and fragile. I was just about able to handle our son when he first came along. Even though the midwives assured me that babies are 'tough little things', I didn't feel all that reassured. I was more confident when our daughter was born, but not much.

Before the excitement of the visits from the shepherds and wise men had properly worn off, Mary and Joseph had to steel themselves to travel about twenty miles north to Jerusalem with their tiny baby. This may well have been their first public appearance since the controversial birth of Jesus. It must have taken tremendous courage to go to Jerusalem, the religious capital, especially because they were to present the baby boy at the temple, which stood as a powerful symbol of Jewish orthodoxy.

Pasting the gospel narratives together to make a harmonious whole is a complex task but we must assume that at this stage Herod was anxiously awaiting the return of the wise men and was desperately on the lookout for the predicted new king. It would be a few months yet before the threat from Herod would become so great that Mary and Joseph would be advised to leave Bethlehem to hide in Egypt until Herod's death, and some time before Herod would order all male children under two to be killed. But one thing is clear from the Gospels: Jerusalem wasn't a safe place for Joseph, Mary and the baby Jesus to be.

Herod was a paranoid king so we mustn't give him too many marks for spiritual insight. But even he knew that something quite extraordinary was taking place. Perhaps if shepherds had come to tell him about a new king he would have treated it as a royal joke. But not wise men from the East. The news troubled him greatly, but he wasn't the only one; the people in Jerusalem were equally disturbed by it, and joined Herod in the hunt for the new king the wise men spoke about (Matthew 2:3–4).

The predictions about the small bundle of life sent shock waves throughout Herod's palace, the High Priest's courts and the streets of Jerusalem. If the rumour of a rival king was true, then everybody would be affected by it. Herod could lose his throne. Even if this were a bogus king, any news reaching Rome about an alternative ruler would be bad news for the political and economic life of Jerusalem at a time when things were going well for the privileged pillars of the community. Even the businessmen in the market-places and the temple courts would see this as an unwelcome development. Herod and the people in Jerusalem weren't afraid of a baby; they were afraid of a king.

Mary's dependent child was more than a helpless baby; he was a king in waiting. It didn't take Mary and Joseph long to recognise that his was the cradle that would rock the world. And yet, thirty-three days after the birth of Jesus, the young couple walked into the shadow of Herod's temple to present their baby to the Lord.

Simeon was a devout old man who met Jesus in the temple, for the first and probably the last time, when the baby was just one month old (Luke 2:25–35). We don't know that much about Simeon but evidently he wasn't all that nervous about holding small babies. It seems that this godly and patient man intercepted Mary's baby before the little family could get through their legal duties. Without waiting for an invitation, Simeon scooped the child out of his parents' arms and offered one of the most moving tributes to the person of God's Son in the New Testament. He called Jesus 'salvation . . . a light for revelation . . . and a glory'.

Before he was through, a faithful and prayerful widow named Anna joined in the adulation. Both Simeon and Anna had eyes of faith that saw in Mary's baby far more than a helpless infant. They both understood that there in the temple with them was a very important person in a small parcel.

A friend of mine once said that whenever God has a job to do he has a baby. This is a somewhat sweeping statement, but it does have a great deal of truth in it. That was certainly God's approach to things when he wanted to bring the suffering people of Israel out from the bondage of slavery in Egypt – Exodus 2:1–11 records the account of the birth of Moses. God sent an angel to announce the birth of Samson at a time of great oppression (Judges 13:3–5), and granted Hannah's prayer for a son by giving her Samuel at a time when God's word was very rare (1 Samuel 3:1).

Curiously, God shows little interest in ready-made solutions to big problems. If he is to undo four hundred years of slavery, break the oppression of the Philistine occupation of Israel, or put an end to a corrupt priesthood, he is quite happy to get things going with a baby. Usually he acted with the co-operation of people who had an ability to see God's potential in small beginnings.

Moses' parents, for example, detected that 'he was no ordinary child' (Acts 7:20; Hebrews 11:23). There was evidently a rare beauty in baby Moses which made them defy Pharaoh's command. Before history set him apart as a great leader his parents saw something exceptional in him (Exodus 2:2). This awareness drove them to take creative risks, making a tarred basket to preserve his life on the Nile and shrewdly planning to have his own mother to nurse the young infant. It was all very heart-rending. For his parents and sister to be so intimately involved with their own son and brother and yet to have to pretend not to know who he was for so many years was an amazing act of self-sacrifice and risk-taking. But it was all done because they saw something unusual in the baby. Moses' family were doing far more than protecting their own child. Without fully recognising it, they were safeguarding the future of the entire nation.

People will make great sacrifices when they can see a greater prize. It was probably no surprise to Samuel's parents, therefore, that he turned out to be 'a boy wearing a linen ephod' – the vestment normally worn by the priests (1 Samuel 2:18), after Hannah had given Samuel to serve the Lord.

All this seems to add up to the fact that God pays a lot more attention to *potential* than he does to problems. For a while we may be overwhelmed by a dilemma. God is focused on small beginnings for long-term ends. And so it was that when the time was right God sent his Son to become a baby in order to solve the global problems of our corporate sin and personal guilt.

Making waves

Some years ago, as I crossed a little stream, I couldn't help noticing a wave which almost extended to the full width of the rivulet. I followed the wave back to its source and was intrigued to see that it was being caused by a very small duckling racing to catch its mother and siblings. I was fascinated that such a tiny creature could generate a wave out of all proportion to its size.

God's great promises often start with small possibilities. The story of Israel's success is a supreme example. The small nation tucked away among her enemies was constantly reminded that her qualifying features to become God's chosen people had nothing to do with her size as a nation. One doesn't have to be a Zionist to notice that this nation is something of a phenomenon in world history. Israel's past carries its own litany of failures. No other nation has endured such systematic hostility and expulsion from its own land, to reappear and reinstate its identity as a nation after nearly two thousand years of dislocation.

The whole thing began with a promise to a man that he would have a son. It is hard to measure Abraham's faith. As an aging man with an elderly wife, he was told that he would be the father of many nations, that his children would be as numberless as the stars in the heavens. In a pre-computer age, counting stars was the best God could do to help Abraham imagine how many descendants he was being promised. And Abraham believed God (Genesis 15:4–6).

This is God and humankind in excellent partnership, taking small beginnings seriously and working together to make dreams come true. The combination of God's perfect purposes with our imperfect potential has often been sufficient to change the course of human history.

Many of us can give testimony to God's hand in our own small beginnings. Personally, I owe a great deal to people who weren't put off by my own early imperfections, but insisted on nurturing the potential they saw in me. Converted as I was in my pre-teenage years there was an awful lot of raw material to work through. Sister McKenzie was my youth leader in the early 1960s, long before youth leaders were fashionable within church life. Frankly, the young people in my church then had very little in common with Sister McKenzie. She was a middle-aged single woman who appeared to have no contact with children outside the church building. She didn't understand us and we had considerable difficulties in relating to her. I remember lots of arguments. Nothing pleased us more than those numerous occasions on which she announced that she was giving up the youth group, although it was always only a matter of time before she changed her mind and got back to business as usual. But unknown to me, Sister McKenzie had given a great gift to me. It wasn't until years later that I grew to appreciate the enormous deposits of trust and nurturing she had invested in my life.

In October 1999 a public event was held to make a special tribute to her. That occasion gave me the big embarrassment of having my two children hear all about my mischievous teenage years. It was humiliating but amusing to hear from her side how much she refused to be distracted by my misdemeanours and carried on the work of nurturing me, regardless of my behaviour. When I was barely a teenager, she had me teaching my peers in Sunday school with her filling in the gaps behind me. She gave me opportunities to give public addresses, musical renditions and recitations before I fully understood what all the words really meant. I started Sister McKenzie's school of ministry without an application form. I have known many good preachers and role models, but Sister McKenzie was my one true mentor. She was determined to bypass my imperfections and work with my potential. Whenever we have met in recent years, she has smiled at me and said very little.

I have also never forgotten the support which the Revd Ron Brown gave me a few weeks after my dramatic conversion as a young boy. Ron Brown, currently the National Overseer of the New Testament Church of God, was then our regional youth leader. I clearly recall him gently urging me to share a testimony in a Sunday service when I was barely more than ten years old. Just to be asked was a very traumatic experience but, although I cannot clearly remember if I ever did pluck up the courage to stand before the small congregation, I recall feeling at the time that it was a massive vote of confidence for a small and very inexperienced Christian.

Sometimes I wonder how many individuals line the benches of our churches without taking an active role or have left the body of Christ simply because no one stopped to nurture their potential at an early stage of its development. The eighteenth-century poet Thomas Gray summed it up memorably in his classic 'Elegy Written in a Country Churchyard':

Perhaps in this neglected spot is laid
Some heart once pregnant with celestial fire;
Hands that the rod of empire might have swayed,
Or waked to ecstasy the living lyre.

Our homes, nations and churches are filled with 'neglected spots' where people with potential have been passed by or overlooked, simply because they didn't at first seem very promising. That was true of the painter Vincent Van Gogh. His was a tragic story of neglected potential. The young Van Gogh had aspirations to be a preacher. Having trained unsuccessfully to become a Methodist minister, and after a short time working as an itinerant evangelist, the young man turned his back on the Church forever. His painting 'Still Life with Open Bible, Candlestick and Novel', with a dark heavy Bible open at Isaiah 53 next to a light, well-worn copy of Zola's *Joie de Vivre,* tells its own story of unfulfilled dreams and spiritual potential.

Why did Jesus find children so irresistible? Was it because in each of them he could see possibilities for the future? 'Let the children alone, don't prevent them from coming to me,' he said, 'God's kingdom is made up of people like these' (Matthew 19:14, *The Message*). In the vulnerability of young children, Jesus was able to see possibilities.

In 1903 Wilbur and Orville Wright took their flying machine into an open field. *Flyer 1* was to be the first heavier-than-air, machine-powered vehicle to leave the ground. It had been a hard slog with a lot of scepticism to overcome. When the Wright brothers began their precarious experiments to fly their mechanical contraption they were the butt of much ridicule. It seemed unlikely that they would get a machine heavier than air to defy the laws of gravity. Their first flight lasted only eleven minutes. The taunts didn't stop there. Someone asked, 'What good is it?' They responded with an even better question. 'What good is a newborn baby?'

41

No one wants a baby to stay a baby forever. A newborn baby is of little real value unless you appreciate its potential beyond the dependency of the cradle. The God of the cradle is also the God of possibilities. That is why the cradle is so important in this respect. When God is in the equation it is always unwise to despise 'the day of small things' (Zechariah 4:10).

The midwife was quite right to tell me that babies were 'tough little things'. Small babies are vulnerable but not necessarily weak. Apparently insignificant things should never be underestimated.

One night in October 1987, Britain was literally taken by storm. Everyone was shocked to wake up to a country savaged by a hurricane that had destroyed six of the seven oak trees in Sevenoaks, had taken lives and had virtually brought the nation to a standstill. As the pastor of a small congregation in the East End of London, I made my way through the debris of fallen trees and wrecked vehicles to our little church, which had been erected two years earlier. I approached the building anticipating serious damage, but I was pleasantly surprised to find that the place was completely unscathed. I went to the back of the site to see if anything had happened to our neighbour's property adjoining our parking area. Trees from next door had been brought down. As I was about to walk away from the boundary area, I noticed that a wall consisting of very light fencing and a creeping plant was totally intact. The terrifying storm that had broken huge oaks and blocked main streets had blown around and through the delicate fencing and plants. I simply stood for ages wondering at their resilience.

Small beginnings should never be dismissed out of hand. They may yet prove to be far more enduring than we assume. History is filled with many characters who have shown that this was exactly the case.

Robert Hicks became prominent in 1999 as the man who promoted New Testaments through the *Independent* and the *Daily Express*. Most of us had no prior knowledge of this successful

Christian businessman who made the national news. But Robert's biography made interesting reading. As a young boy he was unable to read, write or speak. He taught himself to speak by reading through the Bible and subsequently found work in the printing industry, eventually emerging as the director of a major printing and publishing company. Robert Hicks emerged to show that small and humble beginnings needn't mean weak endings. As someone once said, 'Big shots are just small shots who kept on firing.'

When Emmanuel Evangelical Centre opened its newly refurbished Emmanuel Centre building in 1997, the Christian presenter and broadcaster Steve Chalke was the invited speaker. He explained that he had changed his sermon during the service while he sat and absorbed the Bible texts engraved in the walls of the magnificent building, which had previously been owned by the Christian Scientists. The centrepiece of his challenge was an experience he had had some years before in the earlier stages of his ministry. Steve had been on a retreat for a quiet prayer time which hadn't been working out too well. He had lots of quiet but little prayer to show for it. In frustration he picked up a large rock and threw it into some nearby bushes. It didn't go very far. Then he picked up a small stone and threw that. It went a lot further than the rock. At that moment he felt God telling him that his chances of going very far were directly dependent on his willingness to remain small.

It is an incarnational lesson we must all learn: God's purposes for us may often start at the point where we are still helpless to do anything. Sometimes we may even feel that God has made a promise to us, but is now dragging his feet. When we experience this kind of frustration, we may conclude that God's promises are only as good as their fulfilment, or perhaps that God is only at work when *we* get going. Our helplessness, sickness or lack of resources seem a direct contradiction of what we believe God promised to do. In such situations, promises may seem like provocation. We look at ourselves and struggle to take God seriously.

In my formative years as a preacher, 'God's Waiting Room' was the title of a sermon I often preached to myself. It was a reminder that many biblical characters had a long wait between God's promise to them and the fulfilment of that calling. The sermon made sense to me when I looked up the meaning of the word 'wait'. One definition said, 'to be in a state of readiness'. That was very helpful. Hitherto I had thought of waiting as a passive condition. In reality it is everything but that. Waiting is to sit on the edge of your seat with your case packed, not a lethargic fumbling through your top drawer to find a few belongings for the journey. The thought helped me to handle some of the anguish of my earlier years and to bridge the gap between what I felt God was saying about my life and the lack of any evidence to back it up.

Elizabeth, Mary's close relative, put her finger on it. Mary and Abraham had similar strong points. They both believed what God said before they saw the evidence. 'Blessed is she who has believed that what the Lord has said to her will be accomplished' (Luke 1:45). Mary too believed what God said – even before the birth of her baby, and extended that faith at his cradle.

At the manger Mary had little more to go on than the extra-ordinary promises of the angels, and the testimony of the wise men and the shepherds. Her joy at being a mother mingled with questions about the future. What she had was a baby with a lot of promise. But there in the cradle, Mary's baby was what God had in mind for humanity. On the day when Mary, Joseph and Jesus went to the temple, Simeon and Anna confirmed all that had been said to Mary. Old Anna was so convinced that she spoke about him to everyone who looked for the promise (Luke 2:38). They all understood that God's promises hold true, even at the baby stage.

When we think about the cradle in which Jesus's life on earth began, we should remember that God's purposes usually start small and grow up with us. God can do things swiftly but usually he grows our potential over long periods of time. And in the process, almost certainly there will be temptations in the wilderness and opposition from those who claim to speak in God's name; we may be faced with unbelieving companions and even suffer brutality before we can truly say our task is finished. But if you feel you are only at the beginning, it is OK. That is normally the place where God starts.

People with small dreams shouldn't be put off, if to the best of their awareness God has pledged his support. Martin Graham came to see me in 1998 with a small idea for evangelism called 'On the Move'. It was one of the most unassuming ideas for open-air evangelism I had come across in a long time. Relatively soon, Martin found himself leaving a comfortable job to follow a small idea of offering food to passers-by in market areas and talking to them about Jesus. Since that time, 'On the Move' has grown to a UK-wide ministry, aiming to have 25,000 people involved in almost 150 centres by the end of 2000.

When the organisers of March for Jesus had their first march in the East End of London in 1988, it was a modest event hoping to attract several thousand people. By its final year in 2000, it was an international movement involving fifteen million people in 150 countries across the world. Similar things could be said for many other global movements which have touched thousands of lives, such as Alpha, that in their early beginnings no one really expected to grow in the way they did.

What we are and what we are doing *now* is never what we are to become and what we may yet achieve. Around the cradle we must refuse merely to believe our eyes. Babies can still be kings.

4
Leadership:
A King in a Cradle

The Last Emperor is an epic film about the child–monarch of China, Pu Yi. The film traces his remarkable life from the early years of his reign as emperor to his abdication when Japan invaded China, and afterwards. What I found particularly fascinating in the opening scenes of the film was the idea of a child-leader being mentored by guardians who themselves were subject to the emotional impulses of a child. The ancient world knew other examples of child-kings. For example, Josiah, an early king of Israel, first wobbled up to the throne when he was only eight years old.

As far as Mary could make out from the angel Gabriel's announcement, her son was destined to become a future king, a saviour who in the unspecified future would save the people from sin. When the wise men and the shepherds appeared at the stable door, she was forced to fast-forward her views about her son. For the wise men and the shepherds failed to see only a baby. He couldn't even crawl, but in the cradle they saw a king.

And they weren't the only ones. Herod had taken the wise men's news about the king in Bethlehem very seriously. So seriously in fact that he was prepared to commit genocide, killing hundreds of baby boys in an effort to exterminate Jesus. The whole affair sounds a little extreme but Herod was an extremist. A great architect and builder, he erected numerous magnificent monuments. His works included the famous fortress at Masada and his own palace in Jerusalem. His masterpiece was the temple in Jerusalem, built to win over Jewish public opinion. An old Jewish tradition said, 'He that has not seen the temple of Herod has never known what beauty is.'

But King Herod was not a very nice man. He was the epitome of a despotic, paranoid monarch. His scramble for power began when he was governor in Galilee. When he assumed the power of life and death, brutally squashing a nationalist movement in Galilee, the ruling council in Jerusalem were not pleased. Technically, only the Sanhedrin had that right and so they summoned Herod to Jerusalem. Having arrived with a letter from the governor demanding his acquittal, Herod returned some time later with an army intending to take vengeance on the Jerusalem authorities but was stopped only by his father's intervention. Eventually, Rome declared him 'king of Israel' and the successor to David's throne.

But the fact that he was an Edomite who married into the Jewish faith was simply too much for the Jewish people. Herod returned to Palestine to resistance from Jerusalem and when he finally imposed his rule on the city with Rome's backing, it was at the expense of many Jewish lives. The people never forgave him. Thereafter, his reign was a catalogue of carnage. Herod's butchery included the wife he loved, Mariamme, and the systematic extermination of his entire family. He killed his last victim five days before he himself died. It was his heir, Antipater, who tried to take his power from him. Jesus was a baby in Egypt at the time.

Herod's behaviour was symptomatic of a kind of paranoid insanity. But it also belonged to a period when leaders ruled with iron fists and unquestioned power, when emperors presented themselves as demigods. The great model of power came from Rome – the political, military and legal epicentre of the known world. From his palace in Jerusalem, Herod did as the Romans did. In his time he had put down insurrections, exterminated rivals, overturned cities and escaped political intrigue. Now in his final years he was afraid of a baby. Even if Herod was mad, he was sane enough to take wise men seriously. And no one is more afraid of power than those who exercise it.

Lying in his cradle, gurgling and spewing, Jesus commanded worship and incited fear. Lying in his cradle, Jesus was a king.

A crisis of leadership

A good friend sent me a copy of James C. Collins and Jerry I. Porras's book, *Built to Last* (Random House, 1998). It is the fascinating account of a number of companies who all had a track record of over fifty years. The study compared a number of 'successful' companies with their closest rivals. The important thing about the book is that it is a comparison between degrees of success rather than success and failure. It noted a number of characteristics of companies. Leadership was an important element, but I was really struck by the fact that as far as the study was concerned, a successful company did not need a charismatic or even a dynamic leader.

Many concepts guide our attitudes to leadership today. For a start, it is very hard to avoid the allure of media-driven, photogenic leadership. We all know that a politician's success or failure may have much more to do with their appearance than their abilities as politicians. The political parking lots have a host of politicians who didn't quite make it for that very reason. The celebrated challenge between Ronald Reagan and Jimmy Carter appears to have been determined by the fact that Carter did not look as good as Reagan. There have been those who suggested that lack of personality kept the Labour leader Michael Foot from premiership. The Conservative opposition leader William Hague has struggled in opinion polls simply because people are unhappy with the way he looks and sounds. When Hague replaced John Redwood with Michael Portillo in his shadow cabinet in February 2000, even serious columnists speculated that his television presence was a contributing factor. The *Guardian* described Portillo as a 'media darling'.

We are certainly not short of good advice about leadership. Both within the Christian community and on management bookshelves we are well supplied with hints, principles and general advice on leadership and the management of human resources. It's just that we are short of good public models.

Church leadership in the twenty-first century is no easy task. The greatest temptation is to conform to the popular perception that good leadership is all about being visionary, strategic, organised, entrepreneurial, charismatic, enthusiastic and energetic. Of course it is all of those things and more! No one wants to find themself in a church, political party or business where the leadership appears to be on a rudderless circular journey of wishful thinking.

Sadly, many church leadership models are anachronistic bureaucracies of endless committees which slow up progress and keep church life in a constant state of maintenance rather than vision and cutting edge. Rob Frost's excellent book *Which Way for the Church?* (Kingsway, 1997) explores these issues particularly in relation to historic churches. Once thriving examples of visionary leadership, movements such as Methodism now find themselves struggling for survival.

The advantage of many independent churches is that they can work in environments where the leader makes decisions without elaborate processes. Better to be involved in something which actually works and has the feeling of 'going places' than to become encased in monuments where things take years to work their way through the concrete slabs of committee meetings. Such independent churches and organisations are usually very good at making statements reminding us that God didn't create by committee. In their leadership, important decisions are carried through by the leader's skills and vision, and with the members' agreement that he or she is the right person, going in the right direction. Finance committees and church conferences don't get in the way of progress.

Some years ago I sat in a meeting discussing ideas for celebrating the millennium. Everyone agreed that the idea of working on a joint project was a very good one. The crunch came as we discussed the budget. Most of the denominational leaders were cautious at this point. An independent leader was very frustrated. He threw down the gauntlet with a pledge of £1,000 immediately to get things moving.

There is a great deal to be said for strong leadership from the front which has an apostolic confidence and which is clearly being successful. But the stakes go up as the size of the congregation, vision and cost of the enterprise increases. We all know that they are great models when they work well but equally they can go disastrously wrong, as Jim and Tammy Bakker in the United States reminded us a few years ago. Their high-profile, multi-million-dollar Christian Heritage Park broadcasting and evangelistic empire became accountable to no one. Shortly after that they were exposed and arrested for fraud. A friend took me to see the complex in North Carolina. It was an impressive display of success and entrepreneurial flare. It all went wrong, not necessarily because it was wrong, but because their unilateral behaviour took them into a style of leadership which looked less like an evangelistic ministry and a lot more like a multinational corporation without accountability.

Personally, I am very pleased that Christians are much more upbeat nowadays about positive images of church growth than we have been before. British church life, particularly, has had a deep suspicion of anything that is working well. Small is not always intrinsically beautiful and it is good that more and more church leaders are willing to learn from the 'mega churches' about ways in which their leadership may stimulate greater growth. The reality is that the vast majority of churches in Europe and the USA still have about fifty people in them and are unlikely to grow much beyond that. It would be a travesty for the Christian Church if our understanding of good leadership became equated with playing the numbers game and looking for congregations with standing room only. God will always be far more interested in the quality of our people and the integrity of our leadership than he is in our size or fame.

We simply must not run the risk of taking our models of success from our society instead of our Saviour. And our society has a crisis of leadership. The mid-nineties were a difficult period for the Conservative government. Finally, a bad track record of 'sleaze' contributed to their election defeat after three terms of office. Since that time political parties have been super-sensitive about matters of integrity. In recent years Conservative politics has been tarnished with the misdeeds of its former cabinet minister Jonathan Aitken, who committed perjury by falsifying evidence to the high court. In January 2000 Jeffrey Archer was dismissed as the Conservative candidate for Mayor of London and the following month he lost his membership of the Conservative Party for falsifying an alibi in an old case which came to light.

In 1997, the Labour government came to power with a clear commitment to be a sleaze-free party. Within the first thousand days of its administration, Peter Mandelson, New Labour's chief architect and its Trade and Industry Secretary resigned; its Paymaster General, Geoffrey Robinson, and Ron Davies, the Secretary of State for Wales, lost their offices as a result of 'allegations' and misjudgments.

This dismal political track record shows the extent to which public credibility in leadership is suffering. On the bright side it shows that politicians in Britain are attempting to take seriously the relationship between private behaviour and public responsibility. The same cannot be said of the US public's response to President Bill Clinton's affair with Monica Lewinsky in 1999. Having committed adultery, lied and vilified the former White House intern, President Clinton clung like grim death to power. President Clinton's political survival of impeachment was a sad day for American public life. It was not that his behaviour was unforgivable. Frankly, David's sin with Bathsheba was worse and he was still allowed to be king. It was a sad day because the President did not seem to think that his behaviour was worthy of resignation, and in the end the American public agreed that he should stay because his economic and employment policies were successful.

A better idea

Leadership is caught in the cross-currents of media-made models of power and a culture that increasingly refuses to be dictated to. There is still plenty of evidence that people continue to enjoy strong leadership – especially when that leadership is calculated to deliver their own perceived needs. But we are also undoubtedly in a culture where people refuse to be bullied or have their feelings of self-importance crushed. The latter half of the twentieth century was less concerned about empires based on political power than previously. In the aftermath of the Cold War even military might has gradually lost its hold. Today, power has a lot more to do with influence and the ability to inform and empower individuals in their self-determination.

Roy Clement's address in Spring Harvest's *At Work Together* in 1998 put it very helpfully:

We are in danger of becoming suspicious about the whole idea of leadership altogether . . . We acquiesce willingly enough to the subtle inducements of the hidden persuaders: fashion, advertising – the media generally. The anonymous dictators of popular culture. But the leader – the man or woman who tries to exert direct, personal influence on us, he or she – finds it very hard going, I think today. . . like rebellious adolescents the only way we know how to assert our self-determination it seems, is by hurling brickbats at anybody presumptuous enough to try to tell us what to do in any way whatsoever.

Caught between the power models of success in our glossy magazines and the defiance of individual freedom, an increasing number of leaders feel as though they are being asked to walk on water. This search is taking place in the Church, as well as the wider society. Managers and leaders are now talking about models of leadership which command respect without crushing people.

Ken Blanchard's fascinating little book, *The Heart of a Leader* (Honor Books, 1998), has a number of helpful insights into leadership. His easy-to-read work holds together such contradictory themes as: 'Think Big! Act Big! Be Big' and 'If you want people to be responsible, be responsive to their needs'. There is an increasing recognition that productivity and performance ratings cannot be the dominant features of good leadership.

Charles Handy, the well-known specialist in management, gives some useful advice on resolving another apparent tension:

> The softer words of leadership and vision and common purpose will replace the tougher words of control and authority because the tough words won't bite anymore. Organisations will have to become communities rather than properties, with members not employees, because few will be content to be owned by others.
>
> (Charles Handy, *Empty Raincoat,* Arrow, 1995, p. 7)

Even in the demanding environment of multinational businesses and high-powered training, there is a search for a better way of doing leadership. Some time ago the senior managers at the Evangelical Alliance spent a day with a management consultant.

It was an important time for us and a very unusual appointment for him, because we were the first Christian organisation he had worked with. He said he found us 'interesting' for a number of reasons. One of them was the fact that we operated on the basis of spiritual principles that we took for granted. These were principles he was gradually introducing to highly professional companies and that were being welcomed in ways which would have been inconceivable years earlier. People are on the lookout for new benchmarks for good leadership.

One such benchmark was given to us at the turn of the century. As the BBC's satellite followed the dawn of the millennium across different time zones, I was awestruck by the coverage of the celebration in South Africa. The camera showed the ageing Nelson Mandela walking along the corridor of the prison on Robben Island. Entering the cell where he spent so many years of his life as a political prisoner, Mandela lit a candle – a symbol of hope – and took it to a small child who in turn passed it on to a multi-cultural group of children. For me it was the most moving scene in the millennial celebrations. The BBC commentators were visibly affected by the event. When I stopped to consider why such a simple gesture should have been so powerful it became evident that there was only one reason: it was Mandela himself. No one else could pull it off. From his long years of imprisonment and personal pain, Nelson Mandela emerged as a leader without bitterness, led his nation to democracy and surrendered the reins of power to a younger man.

In 1997 the events surrounding the death of Princess Diana showed that the old institutions of power could be shaken by the wishes of the people, as the union flag flew at half-mast over Buckingham Palace for the woman who had become the queen of people's hearts. But Diana's death inadvertently resulted in one significant disservice. It eclipsed the death of a saint, Mother Teresa of Calcutta. Like Gandhi and Martin Luther King Jr, Mother Teresa showed that models of leadership need not be driven by power or gloss. Character and a passion for a right cause are far more important. Mother Teresa dedicated herself to serving Jesus by serving the destitute and the dying, thereby challenging those in authority to take the plight of the poor seriously. She had a genuine humility, even when dealing with people in powerful positions.

Peter Kusmic, the Croatian theologian, once suggested, 'Charisma without character leads to catastrophe.' Or, as Steve Covey, the leadership guru, points out:

> Over the past fifty years leadership development has mainly focused on the skills in management. In the future, leadership development will focus on developing people of character, depth and integrity.
> (Stephen R. Covey, *Seven Habits of Highly Effective Leadership*, Simon & Schuster, 1999)

The twenty-first century has begun with confusing messages about leadership. Having participated in the building-up of icons through the media, people are increasingly likely to reject those icons if they appear to take their roles too seriously. Anyone giving the impression that they are better than an 'ordinary' person is likely to be displaced by common consensus. We want our heroes to be as much like us as possible. We want to look *at* them but we no longer want to look *up* to them. We are reluctant to admit that what they do on screen influences our private lives in any way. In our search for models of good leadership we are likely to agree with General Schwarzkopf that 'character is the fundamental attribute of all great leaders', but we are no longer sure exactly who has the patent for those characteristics.

Leading from the cradle
In the midst of our desperate search for good leadership models, it is as though God gently places the cradle in our midst and

tiptoes into the shadows to see if we noticed him. As we read our magazines or file away our notes from a recent leadership conference, a call comes from the Bethlehem manger for a style of leadership that leaves room for vulnerability.

Talk about 'servant leadership' is easy. The practice is difficult. Those of us in any kind of leadership role find ourselves jostled by competing expectations from our employees or members. Most of us know examples of 'successful' leaders who have ten great ideas before breakfast every day and another five last thing at night which they carry over to the following morning! Leaders with differing personalities react in varying ways to the pressure exerted by models of enterprising leadership. Some secretly fear that their followers will be expecting them to keep up with the leadership 'Joneses'. Others, already finding themselves in 'the fast lane' to success, face constantly a tendency to keep an eye on their peers, not to be left behind in the leadership league. Of course, the more successful leaders are, the more pressure they may exert on themselves to keep things moving. And yet for many leaders, the motivation to keep going forward genuinely has nothing to do with anyone else. It is simply inner drive and creative gifting which keeps them on the move. If no one else did anything they would still keep going.

Effective leadership is inconceivable without vision, drive and a spirit of adventure. But even if everybody else forgets it, Christians should not forget that vulnerability is perfectly consistent with strong leadership. When we crowd out our capacity to be vulnerable, we become inaccessible untouchables and less than human. However successful we may become it is usually only a matter of time before the cracks show through anyway.

Not long ago I met an old college friend for lunch. Having recently read the story of my pilgrimage in *Lord, Make Us One – But Not All the Same!* (Hodder and Stoughton, 1999) he said it filled in parts of my life he had not understood when we had studied together years earlier. In fact, he was quite surprised to see the candid account of my childhood years and my unveiled references to my poor relationship with my father when I was a boy. Apparently, he had tried to discuss my father with me during our student days but got a rather evasive reaction. The response was tantamount to a 'no trespassing' sign.

Frankly, I had no recollection of the event. But he had always remembered the incident. My problem was a basic one. In the formative stages of my development as a minister, I was under the impression that leaders were not allowed to have any weaknesses, and certainly if they did have any they were not supposed to admit to them either publicly or privately. Vulnerability was a sign of weakness. No one ever said this. It was simply that leadership as I had seen it gave the impression that leaders were immune from vulnerability and anyone found with it was required to dump it – fast.

It took me some time to liberate myself from the tyranny of pretence. I had to dismantle mental barricades which kept me away from myself. At a time when I thought I had my act together, a friend was able to identify a strain in my relationship with myself.

Of course it wouldn't do to have one's emotions on permanent display. We all need some space and none of us, as leader or not, could cope with relentless transparency. Indeed, even if *we* can handle it, it is unlikely that others will. Jeremiah the prophet had a lot going for him, but few people would hold him up as their first choice for an ideal leader. Perennial melancholy makes us all jumpy – even if the prophecy is good. But leadership is not incompatible with vulnerability.

A sermon on character traits

It's no accident that Matthew's Gospel sets the Sermon on the Mount (Matthew 5–7) at the opening stages of Jesus's ministry. The Beatitudes – the passage we tend to know best (Matthew 5:1–12) – is a perfect example of Jesus's topsy-turvy world of kingdom values. Matthew is keen to point out that although a crowd was following Jesus, it was only his disciples who made the extra climb to listen to his radical message. Eugene Peterson's paraphrase *The Message* gets the point home: 'Those apprenticed to him, the committed, climbed with him.' The fact is that Matthew 5 is not a list of impossible ideals but the character traits of people who wanted to stand out from the crowd as true disciples. When Jesus looked around these were the kind of people he wanted to call his followers. The Sermon on the Mount is an alternative culture. It is not so much a formula to *get ahead* as to *keep* your head. It is not at all concerned about controlling other people but it is aimed at helping us to live with ourselves. It is all about wellbeing.

That is why Jesus regarded these characteristics as the indicators of a 'blessed' or 'happy' person. Disciples aren't doormats, they are poised for leadership. The 'poor in spirit' are not emotional retards. They are the kind of people who are consciously aware of their own poverty, weaknesses and vulnerability. It is a happy state to be in. People like these do not wait for journalists and opinion polls to tell them they are wrong. Usually they know it first and will take steps to adjust their behaviour.

During his ministry William Booth had a group of ministers complain to him that they had been working over a long period of time without seeing any results. His advice was quite simple: 'Try tears!' Some years ago I was present at the opening of a Christian project where Princess Diana gave a moving speech in which she lamented what she described as 'a curious conspiracy to suppress tears'. There is a strange irony in the fact that at the very time when many preachers lament the state of our society, there is still so little room for tears. But as far as Jesus was concerned, those who mourn are happy people. That is because the capacity to show remorse for our own weakness and the sins of others is still an important mark of a disciple. It saves us from the hypocrisy of denial about our own sin and indifferent detachment from the needs of our world. Jesus was comfortable with himself weeping over both the city of Jerusalem and the death of his close friend Lazarus.

There is a time for leaders to be tough and resilient. There is also a time when leaders should mourn. This is a theme which the prophet Joel captures with great power. Joel's call for the priests to mourn (Joel 1:13; 2:17) is unprecedented. Usually, priests are not associated with crying. Their ceremonial duties create the impression of a detached clericalism. It is also easy to assume that the regularity of ritual cleansing and sin offerings would be inclined to make them immune from tears. But without any references to the traditional implements of their work, Joel's central challenge to them is to fulfil an intercessory role in which they are called to weep for the people. It was a calling to a leadership of vulnerability marked by tears. One reason why Jesus taught that those who keep the capacity to mourn are happy people is because they will use up little energy in pretence.

Moses was not a perfect leader. A close look at his life shows him to be a man with an identity crisis in his early years; he was a murderer with an impetuous streak and a speech impediment. But he was also described as one of the meekest men in the Bible. As the saying goes, 'Moses was meek but he was not weak.' Sometimes the two are hopelessly confused. I loved Paul Newman's film *Cool Hand Luke*. In it he plays a rather inscrutable prisoner who challenges the system in a prison in the Deep South. His indomitable spirit is tested by a fight with a much bigger inmate than himself. During the fight it becomes evident that the man is far too strong for Luke. But although he is badly beaten the fact that he refuses to 'stay down' overwhelms his opponent, who eventually carries him away and becomes his most devoted follower. The meekness Jesus spoke about in the Sermon on the Mount has nothing to do with cowering to opposition. Meekness is a measure of resilience that is able to stand up for right without riotous behaviour. It was the quality Jesus himself displayed before the High Priest, Pilate and the angry mob on the night he was betrayed.

The distance from the manger to the mount is not really so far. There is a note of vulnerability that characterises the cradle, which reaches across to Jesus's ideas about happiness. Everyone who wants to follow this king is challenged to cultivate the characteristics of humility that run through the Beatitudes.

Triumph and trembling

'People with humility,' said Ken Blanchard, 'don't think less of themselves, they think of themselves less.' That seems to make sense if we are to keep a balance between the drive and vigour of effective leadership and the call to vulnerability. These contrasting characteristics are to be found in Paul's leadership, for this irrepressible apostle who described himself as a man with a direct commission from God also gave way to some of the most transparent expressions of weakness.

It was a theme to which he returned in his letter to the Colossians. In a competitive culture where might is often deemed to be right, few of us would want to be so open to our readers as Paul was. Commissioned by God as he claimed to be (Colossians 1:1), he was not afraid to admit that he was 'struggling' (the word means 'agonising') for their growth.

Paul was unafraid to tell the people in Corinth that his ministry was with a 'demonstration of the Spirit's power', as much as in 'weakness and fear, and with much trembling' (1 Corinthians 2:3–4). The laws of public speaking say that it is wrong to begin an address with an apology. Paul does not begin his first letter to the Corinthians with an apology but he is not far off. He is prepared to be vulnerable.

The sad truth is that the pulpit and places of public profile are often filled with high-risk people, not because they are not talented or experienced but because they are emotional time bombs waiting to go off. Often the place of leadership is the loneliest place on earth because it seems to be the one place from which people are not allowed to ask for help. Most of us will know of someone whose public failure surprised us until we heard through the grapevine just what they had been trying to handle alone in their private lives.

During the first week of a family holiday in 1992, I started chatting to a man in the reception of our motel who was selling tickets for Disney World. He told me that his previous job had been as minister of a large church. Eventually the whole business of ministry got to him. He grew lonely, disillusioned and tired. But he had no one he thought he could talk to. He walked out of his ministry and his marriage to sell Disney World tickets. He is not alone. I was staggered to learn from a survey some years ago that over 30 per cent of church leaders wanted to leave their ministries prematurely because they were tired, lonely and frustrated. A more recent survey commissioned by the Evangelical Alliance's Caring for Pastors network showed that as many as 53 per cent were tempted to leave at some point in their ministry.

Paul's open admittance of weakness was not to canvass for sympathy. It was to admit his need of others. Paul was not afraid to ask people to pray for him; he was one who generally made his own needs known. But Paul also wanted to make it known that he was willing to share in the afflictions of Christ and the 'fellowship of sharing in his suffering' (Philippians 3:10).

When I was at school my PE and cricket teacher Mr Taylor, an Englishman of the old school variety, was full of pithy statements of wisdom. One of them, which seemed very helpful to my teenage ears, has since rung a little hollow with me. If a cricket ball hit a soft spot or if anyone was brought down by a vicious tackle his response was invariably the same: 'Never let them know you're hurt, lad. It only makes 'em big-headed!' When he didn't say it you knew the injury was serious.

It seems many of us have been reared with similar sentiments which we have carried over into many relationships and responsibilities. Vulnerability is often mistaken for weakness and has therefore been subconsciously outlawed as inappropriate in leaders.

In public life, there is a clear reluctance to admit to personal weaknesses. By common consent, no one wants a 'loser' for a leader. Politics and the holding of public office have increasingly become driven by dirty tricks campaigns as opposed to the real issues – let alone the character of leaders. Personal acrimony marked the political trail in the Republican primary elections for the presidency in 2000. As the *Daily Telegraph*'s foreign news column put it, 'As Mr Bush and Mr McCain were trading eve-of-poll insults, the two Democratic candidates were also engaged in an unseemly mud-slinging match.' According to the piece, the Democrat Bill Bradley made sixteen separate accusations against his rival and front runner, Al Gore. At the same time British politics sank to new depths with political games-playing in the electoral process for the new post of Mayor of London.

Sadly, we are all caught up in a ridiculously transparent masquerade in which no one believes public figures, but in which we are obliged to vote for them, and in voting we all want to back the winner. Winners of public office are seldom inclined to admit when they are wrong. It is a rare thing for a politician to say 'sorry' – unless they have no choice.

This is why the values of the kingdom of God are still so alien to our society. For it is a kingdom in which 'a little child will lead them' (Isaiah 11:6), a kingdom that began with a babe in a cradle.

Mark Wallinger's *Ecce Homo* was a life-size image of Jesus perched on a spare plinth in Trafalgar Square as a special tribute to Jesus in the run-up to the dawn of the year 2000. The first time I went to see it, I walked past it by mistake. In the midst of Nelson's towering column and the giant lions, the diminutive figure of Jesus was conspicuous by its ordinariness. Sadly, it was only on a short loan to the Square. The figure described as 'the vulnerable

Christ figure' was later replaced by a thirty-foot-high work depicting a human head clamped to a book by the roots of a bare tree. It would be sad if Christians disposed of the vulnerable Christ in our presentation of the gospel.

PART TWO

The Cross

For the message of the cross is foolishness
to those who are perishing,
but to us who are being saved
it is the power of God.

1 Corinthians 1:18

If you had been alive in first-century Palestine there would have
been no ambiguity about the cross for you. Everybody knew that
a cross was the symbol of ultimate torture and disgraceful death.
No one who carried a cross through the crowded streets to the
hillside ever came back. It was a fatal and final journey.

That symbol of shame became the emblem of martyrdom and
power before it became a token of prestige in Rome, or was
institutionalised by the Christian Church. As a gift of jewellery
exchanged between friends, the domestication of the cross has
worn away its radical edge. Little wonder, perhaps, that an international survey revealed that the international symbols of Shell
and McDonalds are more easily recognisable than the cross
nowadays.

But that changes nothing really. The cross is still God's most effective way of changing people for the better, for good.

5
A Death with
a Difference

Everybody's hero

There is a general feeling around that people are becoming more self-centred and less inclined to make sacrifices for other people. Gone are the days, it is argued, when one individual will readily put themself out for another. The ground rule is 'me, myself and I'. In spite of the generous spirit still evident in charitable giving and the like, it seems that the kind of sacrificial spirit shown in the two great wars of the twentieth century is vanishing. If we listen to our parents and grandparents and the average sermon, we may conclude that the age of chivalry is well and truly dead.

But there are still strong hints that this is not the whole story. In recent years a string of films has come along to remind us that we still need heroes. I found Steven Spielberg's *Saving Private Ryan* the most realistic war movie I have ever seen. Based on the true story of a small platoon sent to rescue an American private during the Second World War, *Saving Private Ryan* not only gave Tom Hanks the role for one of his best performances but also captured a very powerful idea. The life of one perfectly ordinary soldier was worth risking a platoon for – even if he didn't want to leave the battlefield when they found him! Similarly, Mel Gibson in *Braveheart* was not just a film about Scottish nationalism. It also celebrated a man willing to give his life for the freedom of a nation.

During her GCSE period, I took my daughter to see *Deep Impact* shortly after it was released. The pretext was to give her a break – but I enjoyed the film. *Deep Impact* concerned sacrificial behaviour of global proportions. A chance observation by a schoolboy revealed the fact that the earth was being threatened by a giant meteorite. Its impact would devastate the earth. In response, the world powers sent off a team of astronauts to intercept and destroy the threatening object. The spacecraft – commissioned by a black American president (Morgan Freeman), and captained by a NASA veteran (Robert Duvall) – was called *Messiah*. Initial attempts led to the grand announcement that 'the *Messiah* has failed!' Eventually, the battered crew plunged the *Messiah* into the larger of two segments just beyond earth's atmosphere, detonating the giant rock with a nuclear warhead and sacrificing themselves for the world.

Great movie. But an even greater message. People still need heroes. And irrespective of our growing tendencies towards self-preservation and self-interest, there will always be a place of admiration reserved for anyone who rises to this degree of heroism.

The New Testament writers saw Jesus in this way. Their mission was to let everyone know that God sent Jesus as their hero. Far from being a place of defeat and ignominy, the cross with Jesus skewered to it was God at his best. And they wanted to take people beyond the obvious points about crucifixion to the real work of this unexpected Messiah who plunged himself into our outer darkness, rescuing us through dying on the cross.

But at first, his followers didn't understand that his final heroism would be in his death and resurrection. Initially, they were devastated by his death because they saw him so completely as a man. His humanity was larger than life. So much so, that no one could get past it to the meaning of his death. What stopped them from understanding all that he said about his death and glorification for three years was not just the fact that they didn't want him to die, or that they had vested interests in his messiahship. It was the fact that they had no way of seeing beyond the death of Jesus. There was no way of relating to him apart from the fact that he was really a man. What we now marvel at – the idea that God could die – was not an issue. When they finally saw him hanging on the cross, they wondered why *this* man should die.

He was their hero because he was real. It was his humanity which made him their hero, not talk about his sacrificial death. And even in those last few hours before the cross, those closest to him and the crowd that followed were following a man.

Mary had had many occasions to reflect on this man she had brought into the world. From his earliest days with the wise men and shepherds she couldn't help but relate to her unusual child as fully human. How else could she have responded to her baby and teenage boy? In the temple when he was twelve and they found him discussing doctrine with the professors, she felt the first strong tugs of independence. She knew then that her claims on him would at best be secondary. We can only imagine that his teenage years would have increasingly offered more of the same. But even as he emerged into manhood and slid into his first miracle in Cana (John 2:1–11), it was evident that Mary was still trying to get the balance right. And imagine how she must have felt when she thought it her duty to rescue him from the stress and pressures of his hectic ministry (Mark 3:31–5), only to find that his public definition of family life gave the impression that she was not included?

The disciples who followed him followed an unusual rabbi. True enough, his ministry was marked out by incredible events. Life on the road with Jesus would have been exhilarating. Never a dull moment! It wasn't just that he taught them like no one else;

he was the only man they knew who always had the upper hand on the religious leaders from the south, outsmarted the best legal minds, or raised the dead. In an occupied territory, no other man held out as much hope for a new kingdom as he did. He was fearless with the Romans, ruthless with religious bigots and most people actually liked him! The disciples' training was breathtaking for Jesus actually allowed them to do what he did. They too silenced and dismissed demons, healed the sick, fed multitudes from small lunch-packs and walked on water. What they did as his disciples was far more exciting than fishing, collecting taxes or planning insurrections in dark rooms.

This was unusual training. For here was one teacher who showed all the signs of being human and yet walked through the same temptations they experienced without giving in. Even at close range his moral attitudes were always different. He showed them what it meant to be human.

It was this humanity which pulled them along – not his strange claims about his Sonship with God that they didn't really understand. He may have been a miracle man but he was primarily a man. So much so that when Jesus asked them who he was, they found it far easier to repeat the confused observations of the people. In the end Simon Peter's insight that Jesus was the Son of God was not even his own idea (Matthew 16:13–17). That confession was the exception, not the rule.

They were far more familiar with the man who grew tired and fell asleep in the storm, became frustrated with their slow learning curve, or who was so weary that he sat by a well in Samaria waiting for them to come back with food. The disciples were able to marvel at his miracles and still follow him when he was tired or tearful. Their understanding of who he was ranged from one degree of humanity to another. Before the cross, the reason he was their hero was not because they believed that he was the Son of God. Jesus was their hero because he was a man of God.

To the watching crowds he was an enigmatic person. He was

close enough to feed them and care for them as if they were sheep without a shepherd. They would have been amazed that this charismatic figure would touch the leper, hold children in his arms and risk the displeasure of his fellow rabbis by eating with prostitutes and sinners. He was always in the company of outlaws, stretching the rules, and defending the underdogs. But he never allowed them to own him. It wasn't that he despised the crowds. His relationship with them was clear: it was to love, teach and serve them. Eventually it meant dying for them. But he was never flattered by their need of him.

Everyone around him was a part of the great prelude to the cross but they didn't realise it. The programme of redemption was well under way before they hammered the first nail into his body. All those who related to him, pulling love and healing from him, were making perfect sense of the cross.

His life was the only intelligent prelude to death. Without the incarnation we could never hope to understand what God did for us. For Jesus did not die as the anonymous God; he died as a man of sorrow who became familiar with our pain.

A hero on a cross

All through his adult ministry, Jesus knew he would end up on the cross. His sacrificial death was always the focal point of his life. He frequently said that he would be killed and rise again, and kept teaching his disciples about these things even when they didn't fully understand him.

The fact that Jesus kept talking about his death and resurrection is reflected in the amount of space these events take up in the gospel narratives. All that Jesus did and said during his life was an integral part of his work, but it is quite clear that the cross is the main event. Around three-fifths of Matthew's Gospel, for example, is taken up with the happenings around the cross. Half of John's Gospel is all about the cross, as is three-quarters of Mark and a third of Luke.

It should be no surprise, then, that the early disciples and apostles also focused on the cross. It had been a long journey for them. When they saw Jesus being taken away from the Garden of Gethsemane, they were shocked. On the cross, the man gasping for breath and for whom they had given up everything was no hero. The disciples were ashamed and afraid. But later something dramatic happened to them, and they grew to understand better what Jesus had meant when he had spoken about his cross. At every opportunity, they reminded people that it was the same Jesus whom they killed that the disciples now followed. There was a fearlessness about their preaching and witness which meant that they themselves had totally recovered from their earlier inability to understand what Jesus meant and their reluctance to be identified with the criminal from Galilee who had been assassinated in Jerusalem.

They knew that Jesus on the cross was the hero everyone had been waiting for, and even though it seemed the most unlikely story, they talked about it all the time and saw it change other people too. What happened on the cross, they concluded, was far more than the despatching of a nuisance or a political agitator. They discovered that when Jesus died he did a lot more than stop breathing.

The meaning of the cross

The 'genius' of crucifixion as a punishment was that it combined an act of execution with a social statement. Criminals killed in this way were deemed unworthy to share the earth with others. So they died, quite literally, without their feet touching the ground. Crucified people were 'scum'. That is why no Roman citizen was allowed to be crucified. By definition, a Roman could not be scum. Generally, Roman citizens had as little to do with the nasty business of crucifixion as possible. At one point, according to Cicero, Romans were not only prevented from seeing crucifixions; they were forbidden to even hear about them.

To the Jewish mind any kind of hanging was deeply despised. Orthodox Judaism remembered the Mosaic curse directed at anyone who hung on a tree. It wasn't so much that they attracted the curse as a result of hanging on a tree, because no one was likely to put themself there. It was recognition that from an orthodox point of view, anyone found hanging on a tree had already sunk very low.

Crucifixion was horrible. It was meant to be. It was the perfect torture for criminals because it caused a person to die slowly, from a combination of blood loss, stress and prolonged pain. Slumped forward in a semi-consciousness state, a victim's respiratory system would be severely restricted. In order to breathe properly they would pull their body towards being upright, heaving on the nails or ropes that held their wrists to the rough horizontal beams and pushing up on the small platform under their heels.

When that suffering became unbearable, they would slump again to relieve the excruciating pain in their hands and feet. People on crosses had limited choices: restricted breathing or unbearable agony. Victims of crucifixion could last for days pulling and pushing their way to death. The way to shorten the process was to break their legs (John 19:31–3). Otherwise, a crucified person would eventually die of exhaustion and suffocation.

Anyone in their right mind would be terrified of the prospect of being crucified. Jesus was. But it wasn't just the physical pain that worried him. We do the cross of Christ a great disservice when we limit its suffering to its physical agony. There was far more to it than that and that's what really got to Christ in the Garden of Gethsemane. As Leon Morris put it, 'To dwell unnecessarily on the physical might well have obscured the central truth that "the suffering of his soul" was the soul of his suffering' (*The Apostolic Preaching of the Cross*, Eerdmans, 1956). In his book, *The Cross of Christ*, John Stott suggests, 'If Christ had died only a bodily death, it would have been ineffectual . . . Unless his soul shared in the punishment, he would have been the Redeemer of bodies alone' (IVP, 1989).

Because we find it so hard to grasp Jesus's humanity, his death has been very controversial, and biblical scholars have wrestled with it since the Church began. Early Christian theology found it difficult to reconcile the idea that Jesus's death was genuine with the understanding that he was really God. One way around this dilemma was to suggest that Jesus did not really die but went through a phantom death. More recently, some have taught the idea that Jesus's soul actually died on the cross. This is an equally serious attempt to make sense of the thoroughness of his death. It goes without saying that such ideas raise many problems. If Jesus really *is* God then to say his soul had died would be the same as saying that God himself died. The meaning of the cross is a complex study, but we can assume that it wasn't the calculation of it that made Jesus's sweat turn to drops of blood, nor was that caused merely by the fear of physical pain.

In one sense, Jesus got off lightly on the cross. His physical suffering was briefer than that of most victims of crucifixion. To Pilate's surprise, Jesus's tortured body lasted but a few hours (Mark 15:44). Unlike the two thieves who were killed with him, the soldiers didn't need to break Jesus's legs. On his cross, Jesus had a lot more to deal with than his fellow prisoners did, and his battered body couldn't cope.

Jesus's death was built into his consciousness about himself. It was always there like a critical assignment due for completion before a final deadline, but during the night in the Garden of Gethsemane he saw it coming with renewed clarity, and it was frightening. Jesus's prayer in the garden was the first of his to seem like a one-way conversation. It was the first time in all his life that he sounded uncertain about anything – and his disciples were too tired to pick it up. No wonder he felt alone.

Jesus emerged from his agonising prayer in the garden into the hands of a lynch mob. Apart from their anger, all they had was

Judas, Jesus's treasurer. It was really a desperate act to capture Jesus, but once they committed themselves they had to go the whole way. They had to find a good reason. To let Jesus go at this point would have been even more insane. In any case, although Jesus visited Jerusalem often, it wasn't a place in which he stayed overnight (Luke 21:37). Indeed, he wasn't that well known there and few of the Jerusalem residents in the city had known who he was when he had made his triumphant entry a few days earlier (Matthew 21:10–11).

In the confusion that night the chief priests and Sanhedrin couldn't get any of their first witnesses to agree. The best they could come up with were a couple of witnesses who said Jesus had threatened to destroy Herod's temple and rebuild it in three days (Matthew 26:60–1). They had to do better than that, but their case looked a lot stronger when they got Jesus to agree that he was the Son of God (Matthew 26:63–4). In fact it was enough to put a deadly spin on the story they would pass on to Pilate who had the final word on life and death for political prisoners. They asserted that Jesus opposed paying taxes and was claiming to be king of the Jews, but when they dragged Jesus before Pilate early the next day, Pilate was not convinced (Luke 23:1–4). Anybody could claim to be king of the Jews and many did. But Pilate was not stupid and his own enquiries showed that, in spite of Jesus's enigmatic claims to be a new king, he had no evident power-base to back it up. In any case, both Pilate and Jesus knew that the malicious talk about him being king of the Jews was a distorted spin from the Jewish leaders (John 18:34). In fact, Pilate and Herod – who came out of the events as better friends than before – saw the whole thing as a bit of a joke (Luke 23:8–12).

Three things happened to wipe the smile off Pilate's face. The first was that his wife took the whole affair very seriously and advised him to do the same (Matthew 27:19). The second was that the crowds insisted that Jesus be crucified as a political insurgent. Anyone who put himself up as a deliverer, they said, was no friend of Caesar's (John 19:7, 12). It was an angle Pilate could not treat casually. But the third thing was very important. Pilate, frustrated with the whole farce and desperately wanting to do the right thing, appealed to his prisoner by reminding him that he had the power of life and death. In the circumstances, Jesus's reply was a gross act of insubordination; he told Pilate that he had no power unless God gave it to him. It was an outrageous thing to say to the man who was the official judge and jury – and presumably Jesus said it in the hearing of other people. In itself, this was sufficient to tip the balance in the mob's favour but it had the opposite effect. This was a truly existential moment for Pilate. At that moment as their eyes met, Pilate recognised that Jesus was a very powerful person. Why else would he try even harder to release this eccentric Galilean (John 19:11, 12)?

Pilate found himself in a very tight spot. He had a choice between killing an innocent man and causing a riot. Pilate's judgment was schizophrenic. He handed over the prisoner and distanced himself from his decision at the same time. Jesus watched silently as Pilate washed his hands before the people and told them *they* were responsible for a death that could not take place without *his* agreement.

Jesus's ordeal now began in earnest. Beyond the pain, insults and public spectacle, Jesus knew as no one else did the size of the task he was about to undertake. Even the silly child's play of an unjust trial paled into insignificance in the face of the real work. And it had been a pathetic trial by any measure. Jesus was indifferently silent during his own trial, because he knew it was merely an unjust means to a greater end.

What thoughts went through his mind on that long walk to the hills just outside Jerusalem? Did he thank Simon from Cyrene who was forced to carry his cross behind him through the angry, spitting mob? Did he recoil as they threw him to the ground in order to impale him to his cross? And did he scream out or retreat into deeper silence as they pounded nails into his hands and feet?

Finally, Jesus was conscious of being 'lifted up from the earth' to take his place among the scum of the earth and of hearing the relentless insults added to his injuries from the crowd gathered under the darkening sky. As he bowed his head from time to time he was conscious of his brave mother who even then did not fully understand what had happened in the stable so many years before. Did Jesus remember that he hadn't seen most of his disciples since the whole tormenting process began?

It's likely that all of those things went through his mind for he was clearly conscious on the cross. He had sufficient presence of mind to commend his mother to the disciple he loved and to extend forgiveness to the thief. In a desperate moment he told his tormentors that he was thirsty. And finally he committed his spirit to God. But no one would have had the slightest idea what he meant when he said that God had forsaken him. For in that moment he experienced the most indescribable aloneness. Even though they were accomplices in God's plan, witnesses of the crucifixion really had no idea what they were doing. But when Jesus said, 'It is finished!' everything had come together. In that moment the most phenomenal transaction took place. It was the loneliest work of heroism the world will ever know. No one understood it then, and no one really understands it now.

Not long afterwards, the darkness had grown so deep that even the most cynical bystanders began to wonder if there was a relationship between the event and the weather. After Jesus's death it seemed that everything else was an anti-climax. The main event was over. The local problem was solved and it was time to move on. In any case it was getting close to the Sabbath and they didn't want dead bodies to desecrate that. Illegal killings they could deal with, but not Sabbath-breaking. Rapid repairs would have to be made to the broken veil in the temple (Matthew 27:51). Joseph – a closet disciple and member of the Sanhedrin – was bold enough to ask Pilate for the body (Mark 15:42–3). It was a strange thing to do without the awareness or consent of either members of

Jesus's family or those women disciples who crept along to see where Joseph had taken the body (Mark 15:47). When Joseph rolled the big stone over the mouth of his new tomb and the Jewish authorities later put the official 'no entry' seal on it, there was no one left alive who understood what had really happened. It had all taken place so quickly. Just a day before Jesus was entering Jerusalem with his disciples, meeting with them for a final supper. Judas was still alive and Simon Peter felt as though he would defend Jesus against the whole world. Now, as Joseph walked away from his new tomb, a long silence fell over Jerusalem. It lasted for three days.

Sculpting around the cross

People who suppose that it would be easier to believe about Jesus if they had been actually *there* when the events took place always intrigue me. There seems to be little difference between the kind of responses to Jesus's death of those who were around at the time and of people in the twenty-first century.

It still seems amazing to me that people could have been so hostile towards someone who evidently did so much good. Even if we make allowances for the hostility of the religious leaders who were consistently at the receiving end of Jesus's condemnations, it is still worrying just how fickle the crowds were. For presumably the same people who enjoyed his miraculous work in Galilee and who welcomed him into Jerusalem in the run-up to the Passover were the same ones who were manipulated by their leaders to demand his crucifixion. For these people, the cross of Christ was a fitting end for a troublemaker. It was his just deserts. The twenty-first century has its fair share of people who would be as readily hostile to Jesus all over again.

I imagine that the vast majority of people who strolled by the cross were simply passers-by. The crime was an overnight act of opportunism. It had no drawn-out strategy or campaign. Many people would have watched the events with curious indifference.

They didn't really understand what all the fuss was about and, like Simon of Cyrene, they may well have been passing through.

In the midst of the greatest mystery, those who helped make it happen sat detached from the event. For most of the soldiers it was just another day's work. 'After the crucifixion . . . they sat around and watched him' (Matthew 27:35–6, *Living Bible*). That says it all. People can be so near and yet so far. But their boss, the centurion, believed it was not just another day's work and another prisoner despatched. 'Surely,' he said, 'he was the Son of God' (Matthew 27:54). Imperfect faith, but going in the right direction.

Although Jesus's birth sets our international calendars, there are many people for whom he is an object of indifferent curiosity at best. The greatest sacrificial act of all times is no better understood two thousand years later. A 1996 Gallup survey in Britain showed that out of 1,151 adults only 35 per cent knew what Gethsemane was and 40 per cent had no idea what Good Friday was about. In the same year a similar poll done for the *Daily Telegraph* showed that only 27 per cent of 18- to 34-year-olds knew that Calvary was the site of the crucifixion.

On the outskirts of the crucifixion were a group of men – and probably some women too – who were feeling wretched. Simon Peter led this group. They had known Jesus well enough to know that they should have done better. It wasn't just Judas who had betrayed Jesus. At the time when he needed their company most, they were nowhere to be found. All the big talk and bravado had evaporated in the heat of the events around the cross. They should have known that this was the climax of Jesus's ministry. He had called it the moment when he would be glorified. And at that moment – the most glorious of all – they were feeling the most wretched, hiding and cowering in the shadows around Jerusalem.

Two thousand years later, there are still people like that today. Men and women for whom God-talk is a source of much embarrassment. They are neither hostile nor indifferent about the cross. They are consumed with their own failed relationship with

Christ. They find it very hard to look at the cross because it reminds them too much that they should not be living in the shadows. They will be happy only when they come close again.

But in the same way that Jesus found followers at the foot of his cross who had no real understanding of what was taking place, so today the cross continues to attract people with imperfect knowledge of its great mystery, but who are willing to believe. And like Joseph of Arimathea, they have seen something incredible about the cross. Without all the facts at their disposal, they are prepared to step outside their usual pattern of behaviour to make an act of commitment. That is how we know the power of this great act of sacrifice. When we see it we can be given the capacity to respond to it.

My training as a social worker in the 1970s included an exercise called 'sculpting'. The idea was that an individual would stand in the middle of the room and each of us would choose how close or how far away from the person we wanted to stand. The exercise was meant to show how close or far away we felt emotionally from them. We then had to use this model with our clients to help them evaluate their relationships with people in their families or homes.

There is a sense in which we all sculpt our relationship with the cross of Christ by virtue of our response to it. Frankly, there is little difference between those who stood around it at the time and our responses today. The very fact that our attitudes today mirror those who surrounded Jesus during his last turbulent hours of trial and torture is a good sign that the cross is just as powerful now as it was then.

The death of Jesus was not just another death. It was God's special arrangement for our special need. Jesus was a hero, whose sacrificial death would be so comprehensive that all the people anyone has ever admired subsequently remain in the shadow of his incredible cross.

6
Room 101

Winston Smith was a dissident in a totalitarian state. Inevitably he was caught and imprisoned by the Ministry of Love in order to have his mind changed. His crime was not merely the illicit relationship he had with Julia. It was far worse than that. It was his independent thoughts. O'Brien – his former confidant, now turned torturer – explained that the state of Oceania had three stages of treatment in their programme of 'reintegration': learning, under-standing and acceptance. Winston discovered that in the Ministry of Love the ultimate place for correction was Room 101. As Winston reached the final stages of his conversion, O'Brien explained that in Room 101 everyone would experience their greatest fear:

> 'The worst thing in the world,' said O'Brien, 'varies from individual to individual. It may be burial alive, or death by fire, or by drowning, or by impalement, or fifty other deaths. There are cases where it is some trivial thing, not even fatal.'

George Orwell's *Nineteen Eighty-Four* was required reading for me during my A-level examinations many years ago but I still recall its oppressive atmosphere from when I first read it in 1968.

Winston's greatest fear was rats. The threat of rats gnawing at his face was the thing which finally broke his will and brought him to the place of acceptance.

Like the citizens of Oceania, we are all very different with varying levels of tolerance and thresholds of pain. One person's meat is another's poison. When we hurt, the most hurtful thing is to feel that we are entirely alone in our pain. When we hurt, our natural inclination is to search for those who are best placed truly to identify with us. Because we are all so different in our response to pain, there appears to be no one to whom we can go as a one-stop-shop for *all* painful experiences. We will seek out the right person with whom we can discuss a particular problem, one who will understand 'what we are going through'. Normally, it helps if we *know* they have 'been there'. Close friends who fancy that they should be our first port of call are always offended when we become such pragmatic choosers.

The most painful thing about pain, then, is to feel that no one else *can* or *will* understand our situation. When a person says, 'I have *no one* to talk to', it may not be true, but at that moment for them it may as well be. Such a remark should be taken seriously for, as any counsellor knows, a person who feels like this may have drifted to a region beyond human endurance.

Everybody hurts

The first time I heard REM's song, 'Everybody hurts sometime', I was struck by its pathos and syncretism, as much as its deep empathy with the human condition. My children had to take me through a steep learning curve! REM represents one of the best examples of modern spiritual fusion. Throughout their video, the viewer is treated to an assortment of wisdom statements from a range of religions. But the central point is undeniable: at some time, *everybody* hurts.

We live in a world filled with pain and the old question keeps rearing its head: 'How could a good God let such bad things happen to good people?' For most of us this is one of the greatest obstacles to faith. This may be the kind of question we ask ourselves or find others asking us as we struggle to respond to earthquakes in Turkey, famines and war in Africa or typhoons in Bangladesh. When schoolchildren in the USA are irrationally mowed down by their fellow students, it leaves us wondering. As the people of the Balkans pick up the pieces left after civil war and thousands swell the ranks of over twenty million refugees worldwide, we are left with Philip Yancey's question, 'Where is God when it hurts?'

Theologians have wrestled with God's involvement with human suffering for many years. The question of God's impassability is a difficult one, for if he really is Almighty, how can he possibly understand what it means to suffer pain? But if God is Jesus, may we rightly assume that Jesus's pain on the cross was itself a kind of phantom suffering? The whole debate takes us back to the heart of the gospel and huge questions about the nature of Jesus as God and man. But Jürgen Moltmann was right to point out that the idea of God suffering in Christ takes nothing away from his sovereignty. 'A God who cannot suffer,' says Moltmann, 'is poorer than any man. For a God who is incapable of suffering is a being who cannot be involved. Suffering and injustice do not affect him . . . but the one who cannot suffer cannot love either' (*The Crucified God*, SCM Press, 1974).

The reality of the cross means that God has never been distant or embarrassed about suffering. Most of us are nervous about death and disaster and seldom know the appropriate response to human distress. In the face of recent bereavement or personal tragedies, we often find it easier not to talk about suffering; instead we wander around the issues making polite conversation for fear that we may say the wrong thing or be confronted with our own emotions and vulnerability. God knows no such embarrassment. The cross has earned its place right at the centre of human suffering.

In the Holocaust Museum in Washington, the 'Daniel Story' provides a poignant reminder of the one and a half million children who perished in Hitler's concentration camps. Daniel was a Jewish boy who lived in Germany with his parents and sister Erica. In his diary, Daniel traced the steps of Germany's decline into fascism and the persecution which resulted in the loss of his mother and sister. On the day they came to put him on the train bound for the camps, Daniel wrote in his diary,

Dear Diary,
My worst fear has come true.
They are taking us away.
Daniel.

Auschwitz became a twentieth-century synonym for suffering. The German concentration camp remains a symbol of the agony of Jews and other marginalised people under the Third Reich. And yet it was fitting that in 1998 a new church was opened and dedicated on the site of Auschwitz by Pope John Paul II in memory of those killed there during the Second World War. In his sermon of dedication the Pope called Auschwitz the Golgotha of the twentieth century.

At 8.11 a.m. on 5 October 1999, the First Great Western travelling at about 70 mph from Cheltenham was approaching Paddington Station. The Thames Turbo making its way out of Paddington at 30 mph sped 700 yards past a red light at signal 109 into the path of the Great Western. It was the biggest rail disaster Britain had seen for many years. Richard Chartres, the Bishop of London, summarised the Christian response well in his piece to the *Sunday Telegraph* in a column captioned, 'Signal 109 and the Gethsemane experience':

In the Christian tradition, Jesus Christ experienced God as Father. Generations have discovered consolation in the divine love, but our faith also embraces the experience of Gethsemane.

When God lets you down

Usually, suffering on this scale is not too difficult to rationalise. Few broadcasters will ever concern themselves about the lack of divine intervention in incidents they report in their news bulletins. Such disasters normally trigger off numerous discussions about safety, the responsibility of public services or the need to update technical equipment. But those who pick up the dead bodies or who have lost loved ones will ask piercing questions about God and suffering. These are the kinds of question thrown up by the teenager who, in a moment of utter despair, once asked me, 'Where is this divine Phenomenon who is always supposed to be there?'

In my ten years as a professional counsellor and as a local pastor I constantly ran into people who thought that God had failed them. Some of them were Christians, others had no wish to be. But they all shared in common the conviction that God had let them down. Most Christians did not feel at liberty to admit this in public. It is not the done thing in a testimony service to say, 'I'm not sure about God at this point in time!' But Jeremiah, it seems, didn't come from the same school of thought. 'O Lord,' he wailed, 'you deceived me, and I was deceived' (Jeremiah 20:7). This is a far cry from the man who had so much to say about God's faithfulness (Lamentations 3:23). But desperate cries are usually honest and God is never afraid of them – even if they appear to be theologically incorrect.

People find many reasons for being angry with God. For some, it is the constant and debilitating loneliness they experience. It needs to be said that not everyone who is alone is lonely. But in my pastoral experience one of the most difficult 'crosses' for young men and women has been the reality of feeling intensely lonely in their singleness. There are many thousands of young people for whom singleness is an autonomous freedom which they genuinely enjoy. My experience is that there are many more thousands for whom it is an unbearable burden that they struggle to endure. Over the years I have found myself in numerous discussions, seminars and counselling situations with single men and women for whom singleness was like a great yoke they were obliged to wear. The plain truth is that many single Christians are locked in what appears to be an unfair and emotionally debilitating choice: serve God and stay single for the foreseeable future, or abandon Christian commitment. The struggle becomes all the more complicated for them in church settings where relationships between Christians and non-Christians are frowned upon. In most churches the conspiracy of silence, which comes either as a result of leadership's inability to appreciate the pain involved or the inability to help, simply adds to the pain. If a person is really lonely there are only so many lectures, seminars, special events and singles' emphases they can take. In the worst moments, not even correct reminders that Jesus was also a single person will do!

Room 101 comes in many guises besides loneliness. Childlessness or unexpected pregnancy. A broken dream or relationship. The death of someone we have loved, or having to take the long route to reach a short-term goal. It may well be acts of blatant injustice and marginalisation perpetrated against us. Insults, misrepresentations, discrimination or physical hostility. Perhaps it is the relentless pain for which there appears to be no medical answer, as in the case of a very precious friend I knew who asked people to stop praying for his healing from cancer. He simply wanted to go; the pain was too much.

Then there are those people who seem to lurch from one problem to yet another. What wears them down eventually is the fact that they seem to be plunged into a series of unrelenting disasters. Just when they feel that they have exhausted their faith in surviving one demanding situation, they run into yet another one. It's that 'Oh, not again!' syndrome, the feeling that it will never end.

In such circumstances, people may be shocked to discover that, as in any other relationship, it is perfectly possible to be angry with God and to love him at the same time. It is the pain of loving God in a world of suffering. All of us know that the 'right' response is a response of faith, which defies the odds and puts our trust in God's ability to help us. Most of us start in this way and, invariably, it works. But occasionally we run into intractable problems which refuse to go away with the first few prayers. When our faith is tested over long periods we may progress to a level of tolerance, apparent acceptance and coping that may look to everyone else like faith. We may at that point be the only ones who know differently. Eventually, though, we become trapped, feeling that God has let us down, but that we are not allowed to say so. The private anger builds up in the secrecy of our brave new world of pretence. At such times we may ask for 'time out' from our commitments and begin wondering how much longer we can keep up the charade of belief. We drift along like a holed vessel, sinking quietly as we go with the flow. These are the times when our faith has reached the point at which it is unable to replenish itself. Often, at that place of exasperation our groanings are no longer towards God; they become entirely centred on our need to be freed from pain.

Jesus didn't hold it in. When he felt forgotten he said so. His piercing scream from the cross remains among the most disturbing in the whole Bible. Our discussions about it could last a lifetime. When he cried, 'My God, my God, why have you forsaken me?' was he merely fulfilling the psalmist's prophetic word? Was Jesus *truly* forsaken by God? Was it that his sin became so foul in God's nostrils that God momentarily turned away? The idea that God turned away at that awful moment has been a part of Christian theology and teaching for many years. For example, John Calvin, the sixteenth-century Reformer, put it this way: 'In that hour of great terror the light of God's presence was lost and he was left in awful isolation. He was forsaken of God, that we might not be forsaken.'

Jesus's apparently forlorn ranting of despair on the cross was drawn directly from the well-known Messianic passage in Psalm 22:1. It was Jesus's best way of expressing what he felt so deeply. Certainly, those who heard the statement first-hand totally misunderstood it in thinking he was calling for Elijah, presumably because Jesus's cry in Aramaic, '*Eloi, Eloi, lama sabachthani?*' may have sounded like 'Elijah' (Matthew 27:46–7). But this verse, and its parallel in Mark, on which the idea that Jesus was *actually* abandoned by God is based, must be set alongside other parts of the Bible where it is quite clear that on the cross, God was reconciling humanity to himself (Colossians 1:22; 2 Corinthians 5:18). In any event, to believe that God abandoned Jesus on the cross presents us with many awkward theological problems. If we really believe in the Trinity, how could God abandon himself – even for one second?

But if God did turn away for that one moment, who at that critical point in the history of the world would have removed the weight of our accumulated sin laid on Christ, if only God forgives sin? And in any case, could our compressed sin overwhelm God or frighten him away even for one second? Or was it that Jesus merely *felt* that God had forsaken him? Would God go missing in his Son's most cruel and finest hour? If God turned away at all, it is possible to think of it as only God's gesture towards sin. If he did it, he did it only to make an important point, not because he *had* to.

But all of that takes nothing away from the awful cry on the cross. Jesus's cry was no pretence. It was a real experience of being alone. Jesus knew what it felt like to feel that God had left him to stand the test alone. The cross comes to reassure us that when we feel alone, Jesus knows what we mean by it, and that the darkest situation in which we find ourselves is no indication that God has actually walked out on us.

The cross also has a harsh statement for all of us. It is saying that feeling that you are alone is not a good enough reason to walk away. Most of us can handle our difficulties as long as deliverance is in full view. We can usually cope with short spasms of pain on our cross. A crisis of faith comes when the period between our cross and resurrection, Friday and Sunday morning, is drawn out too long. It is at those times that we are tempted to complain that Jesus only had three days, whereas we have three or thirty years. Friday can be hard to deal with when Sunday morning appears postponed until further notice. This is when our cross becomes unbearable and God is accused of unreasonable behaviour.

The real issue was not how *long* Jesus suffered on the cross but how *real* it was. In that moment Jesus experienced *qualitative death* to such an extent that no negative experience known to us escaped the gravitational pull of the cross. His death plunged him into such an eternity of death that no pain was left untouched by it. This was the purpose of the cross.

I remember visiting a small chapel in Penzance some years ago during a family holiday. As I wandered around the building, I came across an inscription dedicated to someone who had been 'perfected in grace through a long and protracted affliction'. A great epitaph, I thought; probably an unusual man too. For few of us truly 'fill up' the sufferings of Christ, as Paul would say (Colossians 1:24). At a time in the Church's life when many thousands are still persecuted for their faith in Jesus, it is still shocking just how alien the idea of suffering is in the Western approach to the Easter event. Our ability to survive times of testing depends a great deal on the extent to which we recognise that God is always with us in our pain and that the essence of our suffering is the feeling of being 'Godforsaken'. In the place of suffering, we may join the thief in heaping insults on Jesus, or we may join his companion by asking for help.

Thomas Dorsey, the black songwriter, told the story of the evening he finished an evangelistic meeting to be greeted with the news that his wife had died in childbirth many miles away. His first response was to curse God for his failure to look after his family while he was involved in ministry. He used a few strong adjectives to describe his feelings about God. Someone chided him sensitively, and said that God was a precious Lord. 'Believe it or not,' said Dorsey, 'I started singing right there and then.' His 'Precious Lord, take my hand' became the most published gospel song of the twentieth century.

C.S. Lewis wrote: 'Try to exclude the possibility of suffering which the order of nature and the existence of free-will involve and you find that you have excluded life itself' (*The Problem of Pain*). The cross is no contradiction to the question of human suffering. Far from an indication of God's passivity, it helps us deal with the inevitability of suffering. It does not pretend pain does not exist. It will not keep quiet in the face of human tragedy. More than that, it refuses to be nudged away from any kind of suffering. When we have finished our philosophical discussions about God's guilt in natural disasters, we must still face up to our behaviour as free beings. God cannot be blamed for our crimes of rape, murders of passion, or the pain which comes from broken covenants. But even here, God will not be excluded.

Don't worry about it

We all have different horror stories crouching in our mental cupboards. For some, our worst nightmare is caused by the fear of a particular sickness which has afflicted and claimed the lives of our parents. We may fear losing a limb, or some terrible disaster affecting our children, or our business going bust. Sometimes our fear is no more than our foreboding about the future. Perhaps like Winston Smith in Orwell's Oceania, it amounts to a 'foreknowledge of pain' – just knowing what's coming up around the corner. It is likely that we all have a 'Room 101'.

When Job lost his children and his wealth that was bad enough. The last straw was his debilitating and inexplicable illness; then his wife walked out on him. His family, his possessions, his health – all were significant parts of Job's life. The very fact that he diligently prayed for his children, offering sacrifices daily to cover any inadvertent sins, is a clear indication of just how important they were to him. Finally, as his exasperation became apparent, Job said, 'What I feared has come upon me; what I dreaded has happened to me' (Job 3:25).

Oddly, at those very times when we have good reason to be frightened, God is likely to say, 'Do not be afraid.' Quite frankly, such a response can seem trite and superficial in the face of hostile adversity. Fear is common to all of us. A GMTV programme in January 2000 featured a woman who had a terrible fear of spiders. She described her fears as totally irrational, her body telling her one thing and her mind telling her another. For many Christians, fear is a matter of your *mind* telling you one thing and your *faith* telling you another.

When we are afraid, people encourage us not to worry for a number of reasons. Anyone who hears about our problem and knows that it is unlikely to have the slightest impact on their own situation is likely to tell us, 'Don't worry about it.' They are gloriously indifferent. Some others may tell us not to worry because they have no real understanding of our problem. We know intuitively that they have no real grasp of our dilemma. Others still tell us not to worry because they genuinely know we will be OK. And usually, they know this because they have 'been there'.

Having 'been there' makes all the difference. It doesn't need words. When someone really understands us it is likely to be because they too have known comparable torment which has prepared them to sit quietly with us in our darkness.

Like millions around the world I watched, in February 2000, as the people of Mozambique stood on their rooftops and in trees waiting to be whisked away by helicopters from the rising flood-waters. The disaster that swept away farms and towns causing hundreds of deaths and destabilising this struggling Southern

African country meant a great deal to me. For only a few weeks earlier, I had visited some of the very spots around the capital Maputo which were covered over by the deluge.

It was perfectly right that the Church, which contributed to South African apartheid, should also have played a central role in unravelling and dismantling such an unjust system. Good news abhors injustice but does not fear it. Sooner or later, the gospel will call for justice and righteousness (Amos 5:24). 'As long as there is one man who should be free, as long as slums and ghettos exist, as long as the colour of a man's skin is his prison,' said Billy Graham, 'there must be divine discontent.'

Jesus's cross was not just about *his* suffering. It was God's way of saying, 'I've been there.' The cross, like the cradle, is his badge of identification with the rest of us. His death was the ontological suffering of humankind. In other words, *his* death is the one-stop-shop for all human misery and pain. There is no experience of suffering that was not embraced by the cross. If this is not true then the cross is meaningless. In the cross God presents himself in Christ as our champion. Because the cross militates against all suffering, it means that God will work actively for the freedom of all those who suffer. This is why, far from defeat and despair, the cross is God's ultimate banner of triumph. Frankly though, it does not mean that he will always rescue us from our pain. But it *does* mean that no one can look at the cross and say, 'God doesn't understand.' He has been to Room 101.

Charles Colson gave an account of a visit he made to a prison in Sao Jose dos Campos in Brazil. The prison called Humaita had a number of unusual features. Christian laypeople with only two full-time staff ran it on Christian principles as the prisoners did most of the work themselves. The reoffending rate was 4 per cent compared to 75 per cent in other prisons. Colson wondered how that was possible.

I saw the answer when my guide escorted me to the notorious

punishment cell once used for torture. Today, he told me, that block houses only one inmate. As we reached the end of a long, concrete corridor and he put the key into the lock, he paused and asked, 'Are you sure you want to go in?' 'Of course,' I replied impatiently. 'I've been in isolation cells all over the world.' Slowly he swung open the massive door, and I saw the prisoner in that punishment cell: a crucifix, beautifully carved by the Humaita inmates – the prisoner Jesus hanging on the cross. 'He's doing time for all the rest of us,' my guide said softly.

(*Christianity Today*, 8 November 1993)

7
Comprehensive Cover

It's all very well to have someone who identifies with us, but such identification only really helps us if there is something about them which tells us they not only understand our predicament, they can also *do* something about it. There is little point in a fellow prisoner presenting himself as a deliverer unless he has a 'way of escape'. Identification is important but it is only the starting point.

God's divine empathy and sacrificial love puts us in the place to accept what he has on offer. It's like walking into an insurance company to ask about a new policy. It's encouraging to find a hospitable environment and empathetic staff who live in a high-risk area, but it is of little value if the policy fails to match your requirements. If we have *never* known God's help in our problems, it is impossible to believe his word. And there is no reason why we should. Again and again, the Bible links God's faithful promises for the future to his past deeds.

Standing against the Fall
This is the point Paul works hard to come to terms with in Romans 5:12–19. In the same way that our solidarity with Adam brought us terminal death, he argues, Jesus's solidarity with us

brought life. By stepping into our condition of death, Jesus led us out into life. He did this on the cross when he temporarily absorbed our eternal death. As God's Son, he could do for us what we could not do for ourselves. In dying, he saved us, but his ability to save us is conditional on his being God's Son.

The Fall was a catastrophe in which we all participated. Like an endless line going many times around the globe, all humanity – past, present and future – are tied together at the ankle in a giant triple-legged race to reach God's standard for us. The first one fell and many years later we are still falling in solidarity. It makes no difference that we never shook hands with him. We are tied by the ankle in the same line.

The key Bible verse on the Fall goes like this: 'for all have sinned and fall short of the glory of God' (Romans 3:23). The prevailing culture of individuality struggles to make sense of corporate guilt. The argument that Adam's sin should not be laid at my doorstep is more an expression of an anti-community consciousness than proof of God's injustice. The idea that we are all implicated in our forefather's sin is natural when we have truly understood that everyone shares the same humanity. Corporate identity is a strong concept that was prevalent in ancient cultures and lies behind the practice of a new king purging the entire family of any rivals. In biblical history the recognition of corporate sin lay behind Mosaic laws. Inscribed at the heart of the commandments is the idea that the 'sins of the fathers' will be passed on to succeeding generations (Exodus 20:5, 34:7; Numbers 14:18; Deuteronomy 5:9).

Such a concept understandably goes against the grain of our modern sensibilities. But it is still discernible in tribal skirmishes and civil wars. As the genocide in Rwanda and Kosovo showed, atrocities have nothing to do with personal guilt or innocence. People who hack other people to death in such instances do so for no other reason than the fact that they 'belong' to an opposite tribe or group. When the Allied nations decided to bomb the civilian cities of Hiroshima and Nagasaki, everyone involved knew that most people in those cities were unarmed civilians. But the decision was taken because they were Japanese. Similarly, Hitler's ethnic cleansing was an attempt to wipe out an identity he found objectionable. As far as he was concerned, there were no individual Jews. In the mid-1990s, Louis Farakhan's radical Black Islamic sentiments were offensive to many people because he appeared to be saying that *all* white people were anti-black. Individual innocence was irrelevant. An entire 'race' became implicated in black oppression.

My point is not to vindicate any of these examples. The fact that they are mentioned together is not meant to imply any similarities between them but hopefully they do illustrate the point: corporate identity is not as unnatural as our culture would have us believe. It is just that we are selective in recognising its manifestations. But in fact there is no humanity outside this solidarity. To be a person is to be a part of the whole. It is the only ground on which moral connectedness can be justified. No one can tell anyone else what to do unless we all belong to each other. Otherwise, national laws, codes of conduct and company regulations are simply artificial lines drawn across our global corporate belonging.

Human behaviour keeps throwing up traces of this corporate identity. Every society has good people, benevolence and love. We are creative beings and the twentieth century has many examples of human ingenuity in science and technology. The progress we will make in these areas over the next decade will truly be awesome. And this is the way it should be, because we are creatures who reflect the character of our Maker. Chips off the old block. To recognise our capacity for good merely reminds us of our origins; it is no argument against our fallen condition.

We know our condition is indeed fallen because we suffer from a curious inclination to do wrong. It is an imprisonment from which we seem unable to escape. Philosophers' attempts to persuade us that we have grown up ring hollow now. The world is full of clever gadgets that cannot keep our crime rates down. We have laws that do nothing to restrain attitudes that kill.

People who think God unreasonable have missed two important points. First, the original plan was not to punish anyone but to have a relationship with everyone. People made in God's image were already 'together'. We are created into community. It was meant to be a community of friendship and fellowship. If it was to be a true community of friendship, no one could be excluded. God meant that we should all be in it together and the only way in which this could be accomplished was by creating an unbreakable cord of relationship. God created us once and breathed life into us only once. Consequently, our relationship with him could go bad only once. When God made us he knew the stakes were high and yet he still went ahead with it. It was all or nothing. When the first human fell we all lost out. That is what it means to be a lost *person*. To accuse God of punishing *me* for someone else's sin is to miss the point. Any question about *my* punishment based on Adam's sin is the wrong question. It makes more sense to regret our lost opportunity of corporate fellowship with God.

The second reason why we miss the point if we think God unreasonable is a far greater one. It is that we forget that God did not give up on his fellowship plans. When Adam sinned, God was not left speechless. He did not wander away from the place of failure shaking his head. The cross was his big idea and he thought about it long before the Fall. In fact it was planned before the foundation of the world. When Jesus said, 'It is finished!' it was not Plan B.

What Jesus completed on the cross was God's intention to restore our relationship with himself. He did this by completing the work of the Law. Moses' Law was all about God's determination to fulfil God's fellowship plan. All of its requirements – the priesthood, sacrifice and ceremonies – were interim measures designed to remind the people that God had not forgotten. Again and again during his ministry Jesus tried to explain that he had not come to discredit what Moses had done, but to complete it (Matthew 5:17). What Jesus did on his cross, therefore, was not to sidestep the Law but to take it as far as it could go. Jesus exhausted the Law as one squeezes a tube of toothpaste to its final drop. When he said, 'It is finished!' he meant just that. It was more than identification with our humanity. It was the final part of the finished work and it meant that anyone willing to believe it could have a relationship with God.

Dealing with bad stuff

I remember being asked to teach a junior Sunday school class one day when I was pastor in a local church. The subject for the day was sin and I struggled to think how it might be possible to get young minds around such a complex theme. I resorted to an approach of informed ignorance.

'Who can tell me what sin is?' I asked, patronisingly.

One young girl who obviously felt she had a handle on sin was bursting to tell us with all the enthusiasm of an individual who had recently finished a PhD on the subject.

'OK, Cassandra, you tell us what you think.'

Cassandra beamed – but then, she always beamed – 'Sin is *bad stuff*!'

I had to catch my breath. It was the most descriptive account of sin I had ever heard.

Most Christians have a well-used checklist of sins which we thumb through on Sundays. Usually, it consists of a catalogue of sexual sins, personal failings and local taboos which soon become readily identifiable. From Monday to Saturday nights the rest of the world is judged according to our checklist, and it has to be said that most checklists have a cultural or denominational bias of some sort. It is not so much that our lists cannot be found in the Bible, for many of them clearly are and we have a responsibility to speak up against them. It is rather that most of us are fairly selective in our lists. The Christian sin is invariably the sin of omission. Worst still, most people in the community have the idea that *we* are trying to get *them* to do what we want. They have little concept of behaviour which disappoints *God* and hurts all of us in society.

More than ever before, we live in an age when people are becoming aware of and concerned about pollution. It is one of the emerging absolutes of the new century. Schoolchildren are likely to scold their parents for failing to be environmentally friendly. Society is full of bad stuff. Simply put, God's commitment is to help us deal with bad stuff. And bad stuff often goes well beyond the things people hear Christians talking about. It includes racism, sexism and other behaviour that treats people as sub-humans. Bad stuff includes pollutants like human greed and selfishness, unjust governments and un-repayable world debts.

From the vantage point of his cross Jesus saw an entire array of bad stuff. Hypocrisy, injustice, betrayal and abuse. There was pollution all around but from the cross there came forgiveness. There is no greater need in the world than the need to be forgiven. For without forgiveness, not even love can save us. There is no one alive who does not understand this, for at some time in our lives each one of us has felt the need to be forgiven. Some years ago an evangelist friend, Oliver Raper, told me of a counselling service he had set up for the public. For the price of a local call people could phone in for help with any of ten issues from debt and marriage breakdown to bereavement. I asked him if he could tell me which of the ten issues people most frequently rang in to have dealt with. Without hesitating he said, 'Forgiveness.' In my own experience as a probation officer, I made the same discovery. In spite of the popular claims of Freudian psychology which insisted that people had no real guilt but merely a 'sense of guilt', what I often saw in people's lives was a need for forgiveness. In fact, my ten years as a professional counsellor did more to confirm this impression than my three years as a Bible student did.

For a number of years I regularly counselled a young man who struggles with himself and most people around him. Actually, his basic problem was an overbearing mother whom he privately despised although he was unable to tell her so. What appeared to be a very dependent relationship was in actual fact a very confused and controlled hostility. One day we were talking about forgiveness and I asked what he thought God's forgiveness was. He took a deep breath, stared at the floor and said, 'All of us are born with a kind of compulsion to sin. God's forgiveness is like a switch. When you throw it, it locks off the frequency of the tendency to sin; it breaks the power of habitual sin; it changes your relationship with God.' It made perfect sense.

Forgiveness has the capacity to touch us in the most practical ways. Mark's story of the crippled man who came through the roof is interesting (Mark 2:1–12). What was evident to everyone including the man himself, was that the paralytic needed to have his health restored. But Jesus's primary concern was the man's need for forgiveness. In this case, Jesus linked healing and forgiveness. Dr David Cho gave an account of a woman who came to see him because she needed healing from crippling arthritis. He prayed with her on a number of occasions but there was no improvement in her condition. Eventually, he felt prompted to ask her about some personal relationships and in the process discovered that she was harbouring intransigent unforgiveness. Her story came to a positive conclusion when she became willing to forgive and received healing.

No one should make an inflexible doctrine out of the point, but it is worth noting. We are whole beings made in God's image. If God did not arrange us in separate compartments it is perfectly reasonable to assume that our spiritual life may well spill over to our physical and emotional lives. Forgiveness has the capacity to make us well. When we forgive and receive forgiveness, we are in a better position to be truly whole.

From God's point of view, there are two types of people in the world: those who have been forgiven and those who have not. All other categories are secondary. God's bad stuff list is much longer than we allow for, and leaves no gaps in human relationships. Petty thefts and company embezzlements are listed as bad stuff. Sexual harassment, rape and cheap talk about women are environmentally unfriendly, moral pollutants and bad stuff. Human arrogance, political corruption, envy and child abuse; lying against innocent people and hurting others to get promoted; distorted headlines and fiddling the taxman are all bad stuff. And all bad stuff is dealt with by acts of forgiveness. Even though the gospel is old, it still works on bad stuff because bad stuff is very old indeed.

Most of us will have seen pictures of huge rubbish tips like Smokey Mountain in the Philippines where all the local rubbish is brought. Every town or city has its refuse dump where rubbish is thrown irrespective of its condition. On every tip we are likely to find small items which are barely offensive, resting side by side with mouldy garments and decaying food products. But it's all rubbish. This may well have been the idea Isaiah had in mind when he wrote that amazing passage about Christ, 'and the Lord has laid on him the iniquity of us all' (Isaiah 53:6). The text is a very deliberate description of a final point of arrival. When God 'laid' our sin on Christ it was the most comprehensive and final act of discarding that God ever did. Christ became the dumping ground for all human sin. This meant that Jesus became more than a symbol of forgiveness. Jesus actually *became* our bad stuff (2 Corinthians 5:21). In that moment, when he became sin, he claimed exclusive ownership of all human sin. When God 'laid' sin on him, no human sin existed in the universe outside himself.

The death of Jesus was a monumental event. It encompassed everyone in order that everyone would qualify to receive life. There is no inverted snobbery in this death for it was generous enough to include the rich as much as the poor (Isaiah 53:9). In other words, Jesus's death was large enough to deal with the sin of our self-sufficient and independent minds. But it is also sufficient for the things we do wrong without meaning to. Most of us have had times when we have caught ourselves halfway through a forbidden act we didn't set out to commit. Or it may have been weeks later that we discovered how deeply we offended someone close to us. These are the sins we commit without trying, simply because we are prone to do wrong. The cross covers them, for 'the Lord makes his life a guilt offering' – the offering for unintentional sins (Isaiah 53:10; Leviticus 5:17). This comprehensive cover of the cross leaves no room for self-condemnation over old, mouldy behaviour which emerges to catch us by surprise. For even if others have to point out our bad stuff, it's covered by the death of Jesus on the cross.

Holding it all together

There is always a kind of vicarious joy in seeing chat shows where the host brings together members of the same family who have not seen each other for many years. Amid the hugs and tears, there is a gentle reminder for all of us of the people we have not seen for long periods or, less welcome, the people we could not cope with if we saw them again after many years. There is only one thing worse than not seeing our relatives and friends for long periods. It's *not wanting* to see them.

The chances are that one in four people reading this book has someone they would feel uncomfortable about meeting. They are the people we would avoid if we saw them first. And there are many reasons why. Perhaps it was a betrayal, a physical fight or simply a drifting away caused by a misunderstanding nobody could quite figure out. For whatever reason, we are apart. And of course in societies where a third of marriages break down within a few years and millions of children have no contact with their fathers, estrangement has become a common feature.

People who have the courage for and privilege of helping others to repair broken relationships know two things: it's usually very hard work and it costs a great deal. This was undoubtedly the case for South Africa's Truth and Reconciliation Commission after the apartheid regime collapsed. On more than one occasion, we saw its chairman, Archbishop Tutu, weep. And he was not the only one. It was hard work but it was necessary for the healing of a nation in which institutionalised racism led to the barbaric disappearances and deaths of many innocent victims. No nation, community or family can exist if relational repair work is not undertaken from time to time.

The problem is that humanity has been dislocated from God for so long that it is easy to forget what actually went wrong in the first place. Our sinfulness is like the outcome of a very old argument where no one remembers who started it and who really was to blame. We have guilt trips because we believe God blames us for the mess we are in and is always wagging an angry finger at us. On the other hand, much of our education and cultural conditioning is now committed to finding grounds for accusing God of unreasonable behaviour.

Our corporate ills tell their own story. As the early Church father, Augustine, once put it, 'Our souls are restless until we find our rest in thee.' And we *are* restless. Everything seems to say we are going in the wrong direction but we have developed good arguments to the contrary. We are like the child found crying in the supermarket who insisted that he wasn't lost; his parents were. We are trying hard to prove that if anyone is lost, it must be God.

Reconciliation is hard work. It took everything out of Jesus. But in his cross he was completing the work of reconciliation. The cross was God's buy-back, bring-back work. It wasn't just that God reconciled us to himself through the cross. That was great enough. To be forgiven, to have regained our lost peace and looked God in the face, so to speak, should surely be enough (Romans 5:1). What could be better? To have peace with others. Reconciliation does not let us off the hook once God has smiled on us. John Wesley, the eighteenth-century evangelist and founder of Methodism, had it right. In his correspondence he regularly wrote the text, 'live in peace with everyone' (Hebrews 12:14).

People who look into God's face will be able to look into anybody else's. When we are truly reconciled to God we should find it difficult to think of someone else we cannot embrace.

New Testament books demonstrate this. For example, Ephesians and Colossians go with great ease from the power of the cross (Ephesians 1:7; Colossians 1:14) to our domestic relationships (Ephesians 5 and 6; Colossians 3). Reconciliation is a must; there is no getting away from it, for God has also called us to be ministers of reconciliation (2 Corinthians 5:18). There is no more compelling power on earth to bring people together than the reconciling work of Christ. For he calls us not only to be reconciled to God but also to practise reconciliation with others. The cross knows no other way. It pushes us out from the shadows of our prejudices. It cannot play class games in the office, and will not allow us to prattle about other people when we have made no serious efforts to talk things through. Reconciliation is not just a doctrine. It is the compelling whisper of the cross in all our broken relationships. Reconciliation is the best curriculum for good citizenship and parenting.

And reconciliation goes beyond even our spiritual and personal relationships. For the Fall was not just a broken relationship between people and God, it was an ecological disaster. Nothing shows the unbroken line between humanity and the creative order more clearly than the story in Genesis 3. We may have long debates about whether it really was an 'apple' which Adam and Eve ate, or whether the serpent was real or imaginary. Even if one does not accept the historic reliability of the Genesis account, there is one thing we cannot overlook: the story draws a thick unbroken line between God, and all that he made. At the Fall, all the categories of matter fell together: animal, vegetable and mineral. People ate a forbidden fruit and the consequences polluted the earth.

There was nothing intrinsically evil about the fruit (Genesis 3:6). In fact, it promised to deliver 'the knowledge of good and evil'. The problem was one of wilful disobedience to God, albeit based on very good reasoning. Eve's thinking, based on the advice she received from the serpent, was totally reasonable: the fruit looked good and it would make them smarter. There was nothing wrong with that, apart from the fact that God said eating it would kill them! But my point here is that eating that fruit was inextricably linked with the Fall. When eventually Adam and Eve discovered the damage they had done, it turned out to be much more far-reaching than they thought possible. Not only had they become victims of their own folly but they had also dragged everything else into the abyss with them. They were the first people to discover that, ultimately, there is no such thing as a private sin and that privilege also has responsibility. The whole order of things became contaminated from childbirth to agriculture (Genesis 3:17–19). Adam and Eve became the terrible twins who reached up to raid the fruit bowl and toppled the candle which burned down the house. They didn't mean to do what they did, even though they were knowingly disobedient in one small action.

You could say that, as a result of their disobedience, the whole order of the cosmos went 'pear-shaped'. But its recovery remained integral to God's plans. God never abandoned the world and even the Levitical agricultural laws made provisions for a replenished earth. But like everything else, they were anticipatory and provisional rules until the time when God would create a new heaven and earth (Revelation 21:1). The cross was the intersection between the cosmic crisis in Eden and the final reconstruction (Isaiah 65:17–25). It could not redeem God's people and ignore his creation because both were part of the same crisis. To go back to the image I mentioned earlier, Jesus came not only to rescue us from the burning house, but also to restore the building.

It was no accident that, in the middle of the day, the cross of Christ was shrouded in darkness as the work of redemption took place on the hillside overlooking Jerusalem. It was as though the whole of creation recognised the enormity of what was taking place and rumbled in impatient anticipation as thick clouds gathered to overlook the event. If we disbelieve the historical reliability of the Fall and all that it teaches us about the comprehensiveness of our fallen nature, we must also call into question the events around the death of Jesus. For Paul argues that in the same way that Adam spoiled everything, so Christ came to redeem everything in himself by his cross. This is why nature refused to remain passive. The darkened sky, earthquakes and bizarre resurrections which accompanied the cross (Matthew 27:45–54) were clear physical signals that God had committed himself to a complete overhaul of everything.

There was never any question that God abandoned the earth. God has always been environmentally friendly. It's just that we Christians have not been very good disciples. Good news means that God has an interest in the world. This does not mean we must become New Agers or demand that we join the Green Party but it does mean that the gospel has a side to it which we have only recently taken on board as Christians. It means that a mandate for environmental concerns is already covered by the events of the cross.

Get a life

Have you heard the old story about a Texan millionaire who had a special request for his funeral? He told his relatives that he wanted to be buried on his own land, sitting upright in his Cadillac car surrounded by his jewellery and with a cigar in his mouth. On the day of his unusual funeral a crane was hired to lift the dead man together with his car, jewellery and cigar into a large hole prepared beforehand. As the crane operator lowered the car into the ground, a colleague heard him exclaim, 'Man, that's what I call living!'

You may have your own definition of living. But there is no doubt that many of us find it hard not to equate living with material things – irrespective of our spiritual condition. There is a biblical equation about death. It is: death = life (John 12:24; 1 Corinthians 15:22, 36). As a pastor, I was always intrigued by the fact that very often a funeral service would bring out more people than a wedding. But there is also something about death which forces us to confront real-life issues. Talk with anyone who has had a heart attack or looked death in the face and they are likely to tell you that the experience transformed their views about life and, at least in the short term, usually led to a better quality of life and relationships.

This is the optimism of the cross. In Adam we all died but in Christ we get a life. Unfortunately, when it comes to a matter of life and wellbeing, people get the impression that most Christians are on a very long waiting list. In an age when people are attracted by personality, good relationships and life experiences, boring Christians are a liability to the gospel.

> Most evangelism training involves helping people learn how to 'say the words' of the gospel. Little attention is paid to developing a biblical philosophy of ministry which moves the corporate life of the church away from ugliness to beauty. The best argument for Christianity is Christians; their joy … their completeness. But the strongest argument against Christianity is also Christians – when they are sombre and joyless, when they are self-righteous and smug in complacent consecration, when they are narrow and repressive – then Christianity dies a thousand deaths.
>
> (Joe Aldridge, *Lifestyle Evangelism*, Multnomah Press, 1999)

This makes sense of the cross, which was a victory for wellbeing. Above everything else, the gift of atonement means that our relationship with God has been put right. That being the case, we have peace, *shalom* (Romans 5:1). Jesus's sacrifice was 'the punishment that brought us peace' (Isaiah 53:5). Consequently, the peace procured on the cross was more than a legal declaration of our status with God. Our peace is not just a matter of our closeness to Jesus on the cross, it is the result of God's proximity to us. And it was all taken care of because in his death, Jesus exchanged our torments for his peace. The healing which Isaiah describes has a comprehensive ring about it which goes beyond the purely spiritual to indicate a sense of wellbeing. Jesus absorbed 'infirmities', 'sorrows', 'transgressions' and 'iniquities'. In exchange, 'we are healed' (Isaiah 53:4–6).

Peace is more than the absence of war, it is a *positive* state of being. In recent years a number of surveys have come along showing that people who pray are better off than those who don't. Such research has its own shortcomings and, in any event, there is no suggestion that people of other faiths do not also benefit in the same way by such spiritual exercises. Many Buddhists are a lot calmer than some Christians, as we all know! The point is that in a pragmatic world people want to see tangible results; Christians are able to command some respect for a faith which may be able to demonstrate clear evidence for the things we claim.

God did it on purpose

As I stood before the famous pulpit at Ebenezer Baptist in Atlanta where Martin Luther King Jr often preached, and later walked around the Luther King Centre, I wondered how fellow humans could generate venom – enough, in fact, to exterminate a man who many across the world hailed as good. King, Gandhi, Kennedy and a host of other names have become legendary as good people who were despatched because they became political embarrassments.

Around the cross, there were those who saw Jesus's death in the same way. The religious leaders had put enough energy into it to claim a job well done as they watched him die. In reality, it was God who did it, on purpose. 'Yet it was the Lord's will to crush him and cause him to suffer' (Isaiah 53:10). Was this an enormous act of brutality? No. Was it, then, a gigantic example of masochism as God condemned himself to death on the cross? No again, because this was God's expression of his commitment for us rather than a demonstration of brutality. What greater act of love do humans know than that a friend should lay down his life for another (John 15:13)? If that was the greatest message, God was prepared to match it.

But a greater reality even than life poured out in love for a friend was being enacted on the cross. There between heaven and earth God was paying the price for our sins. It wasn't just to prove how much he loved us; it was, for some reason, the only way it could be done. This comprehensive cover was possible only through the death of an innocent person. In *The Lion, the Witch and the Wardrobe*, C.S. Lewis summarises it very well for us. Edmund, one of the visitors to Narnia, foolishly placed himself under the Witch's control. The only way out was for Aslan, the great Christ-figure lion, to offer himself in Edmund's place. None of the children could understand the mystery and Aslan tried to explain it after his recovery from his execution on the great stone table.

'But what does it all mean?' asked Susan when they were somewhat calmer.

'It means,' said Aslan, 'that though the Witch knew the Deep Magic, there is a magic deeper still which she did not know. Her knowledge goes back only to the dawn of time. But if she could have looked a little further back, into the stillness and the darkness before Time dawned, she would have read there a different incantation. She would have known that when a willing victim who had committed no treachery was killed in a traitor's stead, the Table would crack and Death itself would start working backwards.'

In the same way as Aslan destroyed death and evil and yet remained the children's friend, so Jesus as Saviour does not distance himself from us, but remains an accessible hero.

8
The Great Impasse

A special invitation came to the Evangelical Alliance office. It was described as a 'millennium interfaith invocation' to Universal Love, an afternoon presentation of different faiths. As it came through the auspices of the Central Religious Advisory Committee of which I was a member, I thought it would be good to go along. Once there, I was in the company of over a hundred people but as far as I know, no one knew who I was or to what faith I belonged. No one took any photographs.

That meeting was quite different from a rather high-profile interfaith ceremony that was held on 3 January 2000 at the Royal Gallery in the House of Lords. The Shared Faith Community event was hosted by Chris Smith, Secretary of State for Culture, Media and Sport. Four hundred people heard an opening address from the Archbishop of Canterbury, George Carey, followed by a host of well-known and unknown individuals from all the major faiths culminating with an address from the Prime Minister, Tony Blair. The whole affair was excellently choreographed to avoid any credal input that would compromise any faith group. My role was to join a multi-faith group in affirming our desire for a better Britain in the new millennium. The BBC filmed the event for subsequent transmission.

The previous day I had sat in the front row of a packed St Paul's Cathedral for the National Millennium service in the presence of Her Majesty the Queen, the Duke of Edinburgh and the Prime Minister. On the opposite side of the great cathedral were honoured guests from all the major non-Christian faiths. They didn't participate in the Christian worship. The Archbishop of Canterbury gave the main sermon, and the proceedings were broadcast live.

The three events were very different, but they all shared two things in common. First, they showed how much Britain has become a multi-faith, multicultural society. There is little point in pretending otherwise. But, second, it was also clear that any talk about the exclusive claims of Christ would have been deemed highly inappropriate on all three occasions. The meetings showed me that the cross – so central to Christianity – is under pressure.

Britain, once a world power – with an empire spanning the globe and sending missionaries to 'dark continents' far away – is now a very different place. The empire strikes back. In many parts of Britain, contact with people of other faiths and cultures is no longer a matter of choice, it is a matter of fact. In Britain 6 per cent of the population is non-white. In London, 45 per cent of the population is non-white. In 1960 there were just over 200,000 people of faiths other than Christianity in Britain. By 2000 this figure has risen to over one and a half million. There are 100,000 Jews, an estimated one million Muslims and nearly half a million Sikhs. Other faiths have been represented in the House of Lords for a number of years now and all the indicators are that the House will become increasingly multi-faith. As Christians get involved in the world of work, leisure and study, it is becoming impossible to 'avoid' the realities of the plural society.

Even if most adults cannot, most children in Britain today can say, 'I've got a Muslim friend.' And that is exactly the challenge for us as Christians, for our friends aren't people we oppose. We simply don't approach our friends in the same way we have related to the people we have met in an open-air meeting or on door-to-door evangelism. When we think about 'campaigns', we don't think of our friends. This means that as we come close to our friends and particularly as we see their devout and disciplined conduct, it becomes very difficult to dismiss their faith out of hand.

Lesslie Newbigin did a great deal to help Christians think about their faith in a multi-faith context. As Newbigin suggested, 'Anyone who has had intimate friendship with a devout Hindu or Muslim would find it difficult to believe that the experience of God of which his friend speaks is simply illusion or fraud.'

In today's culture, religious pluralism isn't the only challenge for us as Christians. Tolerance demands equal rights for everyone, not only to believe what they want to believe, but to think what they want to think. It is becoming unacceptable to settle for less. The unrelenting pressure towards tolerance has huge implications for Christians – and particularly for those parts of the Church that take pride in being biblical and remaining true to historic Christian faith.

In this environment, we all have to think again. Christians are caught between old beliefs and current appeals for tolerance. The important Catholic gathering, Vatican II in 1962–65, had to express a greater level of tolerance of differing views than the Church had ever known. On 12 March 2000, Pope John Paul II's controversial apology expressed regret for some of the mistakes of the Roman Catholic Church. Across the Christian landscape there are all sorts of signals that we aren't as sure as we used to be about things like heaven and hell and where the cross fits in.

Some years ago, a teacher of a missions class at the Canadian Bible College in Regina asked students to show whether or not they believed Jesus was the only way to God by standing on either side of the room. The informal exercise demonstrated that a significant number of mission students admitted that they weren't sure.

So it is becoming very clear that Jesus is a problem for modern culture. This isn't because of his teaching. Most people appreciate the things he had to say. It certainly isn't because of his lifestyle which remains attractive in an age which goes out of its way to defend the underdog against institutions. And it isn't the fact that Jesus did miracles. Far from denying the possibility of miracles, 65 per cent of the adult population in the UK believe in paranormal phenomena. Ours is a post-scientific, pro-technological age, and with the encouragement of the new spirituality it is willing to believe almost anything. It is the fact that Jesus claims to be the only way to God which doesn't fit anymore. More than ever, the cross is becoming an embarrassment.

Crossover

Emperor Constantine looked over the Milvian River on the eve of a crucial battle to unite the Roman Empire. Tradition has it that he saw a cross emblazoned in the night sky accompanied by the words, 'In this sign conquer.' The year was 312. Before this point the cross was an emblem of stigma and painful embarrassment. Constantine domesticated the cross.

When the first Christians spoke about the cross in the aftermath of the resurrection, it was with some irony. As I highlighted at the start of Chapter 5, crucifixion was a mark of failure and disgrace. Jesus took the cross seriously, as is shown by the structure of his life leading towards it and the amount of space given to describing the circumstances of his death in the Gospels. But equally, Jesus's early followers seized every opportunity to talk about it.

Within two months of the resurrection, Peter was preaching about the cross and resurrection. 'This man was handed over to you by God's set purpose and foreknowledge,' said Peter, 'and you, with the help of wicked people, put him to death by nailing him to the cross' (Acts 2:23). It sounded so unlike the Peter who had denied Jesus and run away a few weeks earlier. This was a Peter fully convinced. At last he had come to understand what the cross and resurrection were all about. His opening sermon was no knee-jerk reaction; the apostles – including Paul – repeated the theme again and again in the years following (Acts 3:15; 4:10; 10:39; 13:28–30; 17:3).

At roughly the same time in which the *events* of Acts were taking place, most of the New Testament letters were being written. These letters bear the same commitment to the centrality of the cross. Paul was quite clear that 'the offence of the cross' was integral to a gospel which replaced the Law (Galatians 5:11). Not only is the cross central to human reconciliation with God (Ephesians 2:16) but *because* of the cross, Jesus will be worshipped exclusively (Philippians 2:8–10). The fact that the events of Acts and the letters coincide is quite important; it means that as the Church spoke to outsiders about the cross, it also wrote to the young converts – most of whom were Jews – about the cross. With our tame understanding of the cross today it is hard to capture the courage which this involved for the early apostles. Promoting a crucified champion to the Jews went against the grain. It was an intellectual obstacle to the orthodox mind, an insult to the nationalists and foolishness to Greeks (1 Corinthians 1:23).

But the early Christians kept talking about the cross in external evangelism and taught about the cross inside the community. New Testament teaching and preaching about the cross developed long before Constantine made it more acceptable to carry one in broad daylight. It sprang up and was developed in a hostile, multicultural, multi-faith culture in which Polycarp – Bishop of Smyrna in Greece, and the first Christian Father to be killed – was condemned to death as an atheist.

Offensive love

As I sat in the millennial events I mentioned earlier, I have to admit that I felt very self-conscious. Even in 1990, the General Director of the Evangelical Alliance would have been very unlikely to attend such occasions. Guilt by association has been virtually a cardinal doctrine of evangelical Christianity. But in each of those meetings I knew it was absolutely right to be there. Until September 1999, I served for five years on the Central Religious Advisory Committee, reviewing religious broadcasting for the Independent Television Commission and the BBC. This is a multi-faith group in which all the major faiths are represented. This work helped me appreciate the integrity of other faith groups and also the fact that we share many concerns in common.

But I also know that Christianity – with all the historic atrocities that have marred its history – is different from other faiths. Its key distinguishing feature is the exclusivity of the cross. If it is ever mentioned it tends to get in the way. It cannot be avoided in any traditional presentation of the gospel. The Lausanne Conference in 1974 was significant in opening the door for evangelicals to see the world from a much wider perspective by affirming a more complete idea of mission than was current then, one that included caring for the poor and being concerned about justice issues, which many evangelicals seemed at that time to have forgotten. But in other ways, Lausanne set clear boundaries around the cross:

> We affirm that there is only one Saviour and only one gospel . . . We recognise that all men have some knowledge of God through his general revelation in nature. But we deny that this can save . . . We also reject as derogatory to Christ, and the gospel every kind of syncretism and dialogue which implies that Christ speaks equally through all religions and ideologies . . . Yet those who reject Christ repudiate the joy of

salvation and condemn themselves to eternal separation from God.

The claim that Jesus crucified and risen is the only ground on which people can be reconciled with God will continue to be a challenge for evangelical Christians in a plural culture. It certainly affects many Christian groups that want to work with non-Christians on local issues. We are often able to do joint work in social care or political lobbying without compromise. But the issue of the content of evangelism and proclamation produces a widening gap, which exists between Christians and non-Christians and also fragments Christians who have varying attitudes to other faiths. Any serious talk about salvation and the work of the cross will lead to unavoidable questions about whether anyone can be 'saved' if they don't believe in Jesus *alone*. These discussions cannot be taken lightly, because in turn they throw up deeper questions about the nature of heaven and hell. Would a loving God send good people of other faiths or no faith to hell? Anybody who says 'Yes' to that will have given an intolerant and thereby politically incorrect answer.

This was precisely the issue raised recently by Southern Baptist evangelism to the Jews. When the President of the Southern Baptist Seminary appeared with the Executive Director of Jews for Jesus and two vociferous rabbis on the *Larry King Show* in 1999, it was impossible to steer the conversation away from hell, the Holocaust and allegations of intolerance. The cross got in the way. It always has and it is always likely to do so.

As our society moves further away from active commitment, talk of our Judeo-Christian heritage will increasingly become devalued. Christians will continue to take it seriously but in the near future we are likely to be out of step with society in seeing this as a legitimate basis on which to be heard. Our tolerant age is likely to become intolerant towards people who insist that they are supremely right and know what is right for everybody else.

Over the past five years there have been a number of churches that have fallen out with local authorities because they have policies which don't permit gay groups to use their buildings on religious grounds. It is quite possible that active Christianity in Britain – at present the concern of a minority group largely attracting only an apathetic response – could find itself increasingly stigmatised once more.

Christians have an enormous challenge in honouring the cross in a plural society. Our first responsibility is to respect all legitimate faiths. This will at times include being willing to work for religious liberty in other parts of the world. Respect means more than a grudging accommodation of the presence of believers in other faiths. It will involve a positive affirmation of our differences. This is still an enormous difficulty for many Christians, because of their own experience and fears of injustice at the hands of other religious groups. We should also remember with sadness that Christians have killed in the name of Christ. Some Christians are quite convinced that other religions – particularly Islam – are a part of a dark plot to overrun Western Christian countries or are some form of demonic strategy. To such Christians, respect for adherents of other faiths may come only with great difficulty, but hostile intolerance towards the many thousands of devout people who make up our multicultural society isn't an option open to Christians.

If anything has caused difficulties for Christianity it has been hypocrisy. What we say has often failed to match up to how we live. The best way to hold up the cross is by living as those who have died to ourselves. This is what it means to be disciples of Jesus. As Dietrich Bonhoeffer famously said, 'When Christ calls a man he bids him, "Come and die."' A long time ago I heard the story about a new Christian who was being encouraged to become dead to himself. 'I remember being unconscious once,' he responded, 'but I've never been dead!' If the cross means anything to us, it must mean that we become so selfless in the presence of others that they won't fail to see Jesus's sacrifice replicated in our undiscriminating behaviour.

The one indomitable quality of the cross is love. There was a fullness about the love of Jesus which nails couldn't puncture. When he said, 'Father, forgive them', it was love. There is nothing you can do to someone who loves like that; they refuse to go away. It is a stubborn sort of love which behaves as though differences and barriers don't exist. It ignores religion so completely that it treats people as people. According to George Matheson, the hymnwriter, it was the love that would not let him go. If Christians attain and practise this kind of love, others will notice; for when we love our neighbours as ourselves we cannot get away from them. People of all faiths and none understand and desperately need this kind of love.

But at the end of the day, we may finally have to admit that there is something about the cross we would rather not face up to but which we cannot avoid. There will be times when our best efforts to show respect, sacrifice and love take us straight back to the inevitable questions about judgment and the cross. Then we will need the courage to say what we believe to be true. When Christians sign up to a view of God which denies judgment we make a nonsense of the cross. We may feel that pretending that sin has no eternal consequences, that God has no anger and – worse still – he could have found a better way will help us accommodate to our culture of tolerance but it also avoids the offence of the cross which has always accompanied its clear proclamation.

The purpose of the cross isn't to *cause* offence, but the cross cannot be protected from offending. For the same Christ who identifies with us and reconciles us back to God is also a stumbling block. The art of *this* offence is that it is eclipsed by love.

PART THREE
The Empty Tomb

. . . and who through the Spirit of holiness
was declared with power to be the Son of God,
by his resurrection from the dead:
Jesus Christ our Lord.

Romans 1:4

One thing separates fact from fiction. Facts are true. Fiction, however, has a way of stretching our capacities and suspending the normal rules of nature. Curiously, we are able to wander into the world of fiction without losing our sense of reality. If you like, we are emotionally and intellectually amphibians, made to breathe naturally in the world of the incredible, without losing touch with reality.

But imagine a story where the incredible becomes one with the credible. That is the story of the resurrection.

9
Hoping against Hope

Lazarus the billboard

Jesus was at least a day's journey away from some of his best friends: Mary, Martha and their brother Lazarus. Someone brought him some bad news: Lazarus was very sick. One look at the agitated messenger and Jesus knew it was serious as they had taken the trouble to send him all this way. Even the message was loaded: 'Lord, the one you love is sick' (John 11:3). It was all calculated to get Jesus moving. But he did the very opposite. Jesus was so laid back and quietly confident that he reassured everyone that Lazarus's sickness would not end in death. The messenger must have been shocked to find Lazarus already dead when he got back to the little village of Bethany where Mary and Martha were at their wits' end. What could he possibly say to them about Jesus's attitude? Had he misunderstood when Jesus had said everything would be all right? Was Jesus getting tired or had he simply told a lie? Lazarus was dead and it seemed that their one hope turned out to be false.

By the time news reached Martha and Mary that Jesus was in the area at last, Lazarus had been dead for four whole days. It wasn't just that Lazarus had died – that was bad enough. But the fact that Jesus made no response was devastating. It wouldn't have been so bad had he turned up the day after the messenger came back – but two whole days! And even if he just failed to make it, that would have been enough to show his interest and friendship. This was the one he loved.

Now Martha heard that he was on the outskirts of the small village, which had come to a standstill in mourning. Always the practical one, she ran out to meet him. No formal greetings or warm hugs, but a distraught and hopeless Martha. 'Lord, if you had been here my brother would still be alive!' she screamed. She had been eager to tell him that; it was the most important truth of the past four days. While Jesus engaged her in a conversation about resurrection, in some ways she couldn't really get past the hopelessness of their situation. She knew there would be a resurrection in the distant future, and she made her hugely significant declaration about Jesus: 'I believe that you are the Christ' (John 11:27), to be paralleled only by Peter in the Gospel narratives. But Martha did not know how that reality would work out in her very painful present situation. Then Martha, not Jesus, took the initiative to go back to the village to fetch her distressed sister. Jesus stayed in the same place (John 11:30).

As soon as Mary heard that Jesus was asking for her she sped off to meet him with all the mourners trailing behind. 'Lord, if you had been here . . .' There was no doubting it now; this was all they had been talking about since the messenger came back. When they saw Jesus, devotion, disappointment and disillusionment mingled together. They were well and truly stuck in the past. 'If only you had been here . . .'

When Jesus asked them to remove the stone, it must have taken some courage and they probably did it out of desperation as much as resignation. What harm would it do, anyway? But they had also come to notice something quite strange happening to Jesus: a kind of angry intensity which made him cry in a way they had not seen before. Even the disciples took special note and the messenger looking on in the crowd recognised a very different mood from the laid-back attitude he had left Jesus in by the Jordan a few days before.

So they took away the stone that had been covering the tomb and held their breath. But Jesus didn't hold his breath. While they cowered from the stench, he became very assertive. Above the murmur of the mourners he shouted Lazarus's name. Lazarus had never been called like that before. Within moments, they heard shuffling sounds in the darkness and out of the tomb the body of the man they had wrapped after his death emerged into the sunlight. 'Turn him loose' – Jesus had calmed down now – 'and let him walk free.' It was an amazing incident with amazing results, for some of the people believed in Jesus and others were inspired to kill him and Lazarus (see John 11:45; 12:10).

It was far more incredible that anyone at the tomb realised. What was at stake was more than Mary and Martha's joy. It all happened 'for God's glory so that God's Son may be glorified through it' (John 11:4). It was not just that Lazarus had been raised. Jesus raised other people such as Jairus's daughter (Mark 5:42) and the widow's son in the town of Nain (Luke 7:15). There was a very important lesson to be drawn from this event, for until this time, no one had ever been dead to the point of decomposition and brought back to life. Jesus deliberately stayed away from the dying man to illustrate 'God's glory'. In Jesus's day there was a school of suspicion which taught that a dead person may even have been resuscitated up to three days after death. The belief went that during this period the spirit of the deceased would be suspended in the hope that it might be reunited with the body. After that it was hopeless. A man dead for four days was well and truly dead. And you knew that because the body stank. There was no way back from a decomposed heart. But if putrefied eardrums responded to their owner's familiar name, God obviously wanted us all to hear something special.

This story about Jesus's friend was a giant billboard saying

'*Nothing is hopeless!*' But it was also a preview of what was soon to happen to Jesus. Jesus did not cry because he was sorry about Lazarus's death. There would have been very little need if he knew he was about to bring him back to life.

It was his anticipated confrontation with death itself which really moved him. Jesus was about to deal with the final tyrant, death. It was as though, outside Lazarus's tomb, he had already entered into death, absorbing its anger and devastation. When Lazarus came out he walked out of the place Jesus himself was soon to visit. So Jesus's unusual response was more than an emotion of the moment. Lazarus went deep into death but it really didn't matter. When his decomposed body was restored it was a demonstration of what resurrection is all about. As far as God is concerned four days may as well be four years. What Jesus did for Lazarus was what God will do to everyone.

Jesus the signpost

Christ's death is inseparable from his resurrection. There is no truth in the fanciful idea that the devil tricked him onto the cross or that hell threw a party to celebrate the event. More than anyone else, Satan knew he was in trouble when Jesus said, 'It is finished!' Having done everything in his power to keep Christ from the cross, it was beyond his ability to influence the plan of salvation from that moment on. If God took any 'risks' with this plan they were all in the lead-up to the cross. Jesus had genuine freedom not to be crucified. In the Garden of Gethsemane, he submitted that freedom to God and went to the cross. From then on the resurrection was a foregone conclusion which carried no 'risks'. By his own reckoning, God was obliged to raise his Son from death. Everything depended on this, so death simply could not keep him (Acts 2:24).

Christian faith is indeed dependent on the fact that Christ was raised from the dead. As Paul explained it, 'If there is no resurrection of the dead, then not even Christ has been raised. And if

Christ has not been raised, our preaching is useless and so is your faith. More than that, we are found to be false witnesses about God' (1 Corinthians 15:13–15). Jesus's death and resurrection provide the main planks on which the Christian faith in personal resurrection depends. God did not intend that we should spiritualise the resurrection. He meant us to take it seriously, at face value. The ultimate point of the resurrection is to tell us that everyone who has life in Christ will know literal resurrection. When we have exhausted the spiritual applications, physical resurrection will be the final reality we all experience. This is the point Paul makes again and again in 1 Corinthians 15. It is also the bottom line of the Apostle's Creed:

> I believe in the Holy Spirit,
> the holy catholic Church,
> the communion of saints,
> the forgiveness of sins,
> the resurrection of the body,
> and the life everlasting.

As we will see in the next chapter, the story of the resurrection poses important challenges for biblical scholarship, but it doesn't mean that it didn't happen or that it isn't true. Many scholars have focused on ways in which the pieces might be put together to help us with the *chronology* of events. But in the meanwhile there is no denying the central fact: all the writers agree that the stone was moved and tomb was empty. Neither can we avoid the clear impression that the resurrection was God's signal to all of us that he is the God of hope. The most important thing about the resurrection is not our ability to prove its historical reliability. We may do that convincingly and with great clarity and still miss the point. The resurrection was never meant to be a theological equation alone. It vindicated Jesus's Sonship (Romans 1:4) and put us right with God (Romans 4:25), but God also raised Jesus to show in no uncertain terms that all of us have the potential for resurrection. Christian hope is impossible without this idea. The resurrection is not about anything if it is not about life beyond death. God's final answer to death was its assassination and the liberation of all of us who fear its power (1 Corinthians 15:55; Hebrews 2:14–15). Even more so, the big challenge, as we shall go on to discuss in our final chapter, is the opportunity to share the hope we have discovered (1 Peter 3:15).

Hunting for hope

God's great desire is that anyone looking for hope should start by standing outside the empty tomb. In a sense our task as Christian believers is to lead other people there. Running through our culture is a very deep note of cynicism, which sometimes masks hopelessness. In an address some years ago, the Revd Roy Williamson, former Bishop of Southwark and broadcaster, talked about a man he met while walking the dog during a rainy season.

'Good morning,' Roy would say.

'I bet it's going to be another awful day,' the man would say.

Finally there was a morning of brilliant sunshine. Roy saw the man coming towards him and wondered what he would say. 'Good morning. It's a lovely day!' said Roy.

'Yes,' he conceded, 'but wasn't it horrible yesterday?'

Despair comes in many shapes. In the early throes of the new millennium, the *Metro* – London Underground's free daily newspaper – reported that families were relatively less content with their quality of life than they used to be. The statement was based on a report from a Lloyds TSB Life Index survey, which 'measures the mood of the nation', and found that overall satisfaction in people's lives had fallen from 6.4 to 5.9 out of a possible ten.

It is difficult to say to what extent blockbuster films like *Deep Impact* reflect or inform our level of insecurity, but the subject has become an integral part of the film industry. The kind of pessimism that permeates society prevents people from finding any real hope.

For many, it has a lot to do with the fact that there is so much insecurity about. This may be caused by our short-term 'portfolio culture'. As business moves further into corporate mergers and alliances, each takeover bid brings insecurities and multiplied fears for workers. Little wonder that a survey in the late twentieth century showed that only 14 per cent of British employees had any pride in the company they worked for. Only 30 per cent felt any loyalty to it. As most of us, rightly or wrongly, feel defined by the nature of our work, it is easy to see just how many people in a consumer-driven society are likely to feel unvalued. In Britain the second highest cause of death for young men under the age of twenty-five is suicide. It is estimated that on average three people a week kill themselves on London's Underground alone.

It is little wonder that children and many young people feel disinclined to watch news programmes, as each day the bulletins give cause for more despair. It might be an update on natural disasters, the fight against AIDS, the global growth of addiction, concerns about the environment or political instability and regional war. Our information technology means that bad news is always close by.

For many people it is boredom that drains the spirit and that can as easily lead to a sense of hopelessness. Bored people commit petty crimes and vandalise property. Couples trapped in boring relationships vandalise their covenants to each other. The tragedy of O. J. Simpson's life may well have been summed up by his own account in *People* magazine, June 1988: 'I sit in my house in Buffalo and sometimes I get so lonely it's unbelievable. Life has been so good to me. I've got a great wife, good kids, money, my own health – and I'm lonely and bored . . .'

When they find themselves in an adverse situation, most people look for practical steps to take. Usually, escape is not the first option. What is often described as 'escape' is more accurately a desire for a better life. Few of us expect to live a stress-free life; what we are looking for is a long-range view of life which makes sense of the stress and gets us through it. We are all looking for hope.

For many people, the natural response when things are not going well for them is to throw themselves into their work, or to focus on making an awful lot of money. The lottery is the alternative great hope for many and, no doubt, it will continue to be very popular in the future. In recent years, a new phenomenon has been emerging. Those who can afford it have become involved in the 'experience economy': wealthy people spend small fortunes on brief moments of excitement, simply because they can afford to do so and because they have reached a ceiling of boredom despite their significant wealth. In Britain alone, the number of millionaires has grown from 6,600 to well over 47,300 in the last ten years.

In our desperate search for hope we will turn in many directions. Six out of ten men and seven out of ten women in Britain regularly consult their horoscopes. It is truly amazing the extent to which so many millions of adults are willing to deceive themselves in the pursuit of hope. In preparation for some teaching I was doing in 1995, I looked at the horoscopes in three national papers for Gemini on the same day – 7 April.

Daily Mail (22 May–22 June)
Brilliant ideas are not always complicated or difficult to put into practice. Often they involve giving a subtle twist to an existing plan and turning it into something more appropriate. There may seem to be a wide gulf between the situation you face and the one you yearn to be in. But rather than do anything big the crucial missing link could be tiny.

Daily Express (21 May–21 June)
Mercury your ruler in Aries puts you in a rather inspired very forward-looking mood. Right now you want to be mixing with younger people who share your rather stimulating ideas. Money is also on your mind since you want to sort out your

personal security. But spending on treats and luxuries is likely to prove irresistible as well.

Daily Mirror (22 May–21 June)
How trustworthy is someone with money? I ask this as you will have to keep your wits about you today when it comes to cash or an item of value, as it could easily go on the missing list. If not, you may be told lies about prices or the cost of work you are having done.

It is extraordinary that the newspapers do not even agree about the dates for Gemini, let alone make similar predictions for that twelfth of the population. The variety of readings for the same day shows how futile it is to consult horoscopes, but people will continue to look for hope.

Standing outside the tomb

Early on the Sunday morning after Jesus's death, as the different groups of people crept up to the empty tomb to find out what was going on, something fresh began to stir inside each person. First Mary and the other women could not believe what had happened. Suddenly, after abject despair and sadness, they had discovered from the angels and from Jesus himself that he really was alive. Even if at first it seemed like a hoax, it still aroused hope. Did Mary have a flashback to Lazarus's tomb as she walked nervously away from the empty tomb with the angel's words in her mind, 'He has risen, he is not here!'? And later as Peter and John ran breathlessly to the tomb and peered inside the empty darkness their world changed immediately. They could have no idea what it would mean in the days ahead, but suddenly they could at least begin to *think* about days ahead again. They had a new outlook on life.

Christian witness does not consist of telling people they are unhappy when they are not. But it must point out that real hope comes to those who begin the search outside the empty tomb. People may be happy while still being hopeless: it is perfectly possible to be hopelessly successful. There is room there for everyone: the rich and the poor, the sad, mad and bad.

Our witness in the twenty-first century will still bring people to the empty tomb even when they insist that they really are 'all right'. The idea is not to get them to escape from reality but to face up to it. Real hope is the only sure way of evading the mixed messages of our time. It will weep with those who weep. It does not pretend. Hope is not an existential trapdoor or a descent into virtual reality. It is one of life's highest ideals, which makes sense of the material world. Hope is greater than the human spirit because it belongs to God. He gives people hope but he will not trust us with its franchise. Because Christian hope ultimately comes from God it pulls us beyond our circumstances and beyond ourselves into a God's eye view of the world. That is the best place from which to see the world and agree to become involved in it. In the words of Chad Gillian, scribbled on the Children's Tiled Wall in the Washington Holocaust Museum, we may sometimes 'go to hell to reach heaven' but it is still a better position from which to deal with our pain and help heal those around us.

It is the quality of hope expressed by the late Gordon Wilson whose daughter was brutally killed by the terrorist bomb in Enniskillen in 1987.

> I have lost a daughter and I shall miss her. But I bear no grudge. Dirty sorts of talk is not going to bring her back to life. She's in heaven and we'll meet again. Don't ask me please of a purpose. I don't have a purpose. But I know there has to be a plan. It's part of a greater plan and God is good … I am sure of God's love for me and my need to love him, because only in his love can we have hope and reconciliation.

Such a hope, such willingness for reconciliation in place of hatred, is not possible without the resurrection of Jesus.

10
A Credible Hope

I stood in worship with everyone else in our local church. It was Easter Sunday and we were singing an old Easter favourite:

> Up from the grave he arose
> With a mighty triumph o'er his foes;
> He arose a Victor from the dark domain,
> And he lives for ever with his saints to reign:
> He arose! He arose!
> Hallelujah, Christ arose!

It was a song I had sung every Easter for as long as I could remember, but this time it was very different. Momentarily, I was totally convinced it was true. It wasn't an emotion; I had sung it before in more emotionally charged environments. In that moment, the resurrection couldn't *not* be true. In those few minutes, the resurrection as a reality was branded into my head and heart. I still believe it to be true today, but not with the same intense knowing.

When it comes to the Christian 'faith' it's always going to be difficult to keep a healthy relationship between facts and feelings.

Nowhere else is that battle for balance more acutely felt than in the songs and hymns we sing. They can take us from wordy theologising to subjective emotionalism. 'He lives within my heart' is great for personal comfort, but not very helpful as 'an answer . . . to give the reason for the hope' that is within us (1 Peter 3:15). Because music is so important in devotion and evangelism, Christian songwriters have a great responsibility to guard the balance between contemporary music and historical truth. That task takes on special significance when we are dealing with the resurrection.

The early Church knew this. The first hymns of faith reflected this and, whatever the music may have sounded like, the words stayed close to the historical truths:

> Therefore God exalted him to the highest place
> and gave him the name that is above every name,
> that at the name of Jesus every knee should bow,
> in heaven and on earth and under the earth,
> and every tongue confess that Jesus Christ is Lord,
> to the glory of God the Father.

Philippians 2:9–11

Doctrines of doubt

More than ever Christians need to affirm confidence in the resurrection as a historical event in a climate where the culture prefers open-ended options to objective truth. In the late eighteenth and nineteenth centuries, the Bible came under increased scrutiny. During this period of Enlightenment, reason became the arbitrator of truth. Philosophers, biologists and anthropologists brought rigorous criticism to ideas about God and the Bible, with its miraculous claims. As the Church in Europe colonised and evangelised other cultures across the world, missions became a more complex business. Old imperialistic attitudes came under interrogation and the Church was forced to ask fresh questions about its message as it encountered adherents of other religions in their own lands.

As a response to all of this, missionaries and theologians worked hard to reposition the Christian Church in the world. They did this by developing wider theological lenses with which they read the Bible and applied its teachings to other faiths. Once the Bible was radically overhauled, everything else was reviewed. Inevitably, theologians across Europe rethought their attitudes to Jesus's life, death and resurrection. In genuine efforts to rescue the Bible from the ridicule of modern thinking, theologians suggested that the accounts were in part stories fabricated by the early Church to add credibility to their claims about Christ. This didn't mean that the apostles were lying necessarily; it was that these myths were just contemporary tools to tell a story as the disciples wished it to be understood.

In more recent times too, Christian thinking in Britain has been influenced by church leaders and theologians who wanted to give us a more culturally acceptable gospel. J.A.T. Robinson's *Honest to God* was one such famous example (SCM, 1963). The Rt Revd David Jenkins, the former Bishop of Durham, caused a great deal of controversy with his outspoken views on the resurrection. 'Discovering the bones of Jesus would make no difference at all to me,' he said, 'because the New Testament talks of a spiritual body, passing beyond death and into the presence of God. It was a transformation, not a survival. Jesus's followers encountered a risen personality.' Leading theologian John Hick, who published books such as *God has Many Names* (The Westminster Press/John Knox Press, 1982), has made very similar points. Shortly before the 1998 Lambeth Conference, the liberal theologian Bishop Spong of Newark, New Jersey, proposed an alternative creed on the World Wide Web. His concern was to offer thinking people a basis of faith which did not insist on miracles in a rational age.

It would be a mistake to assume that these responses have been deliberate mischievous attempts to debunk the gospel. Ironically, these scholars have been motivated in the main by a genuine desire to make the Bible credible and believable to the modern mind. As scholars they were pressed to respond to challenges, such as Darwin's theory of evolution, that appeared to undermine the very concept of biblical creation, as well as to geological and historical developments which questioned biblical chronology.

'Liberal theology', as it has been termed, has been motivated to take away rational obstacles to faith and to make good news accessible in a scientific age. This approach to Christian faith has a number of characteristic features. It plays down miracles, presenting them as first-century explanations for events to which there are no scientific answers. It tends to de-emphasise anything which reduces Christianity to a privatised emotional experience of God and amplifies a more corporate understanding of redemption. In other words, God is presented much more as someone interested in justice and social improvement than in 'born-again' experiences.

The difficulty here is that all the central Christian beliefs are based on miraculous events. The Bible starts with the beginning of the beginning, by presenting God as the source of life itself. Thereafter, the whole story of salvation depends on a series of miracles. God's promise to give Abraham and Sarah a son (Genesis 17), the escape from Egypt (Exodus 13) and so many of the events in the lives of the prophets were substantially the same as the events surrounding the life of Jesus. They all claimed to be miraculous. The Bible is one embarrassing litany of miracles! There is simply no way around it. And the greatest of these miracles is Jesus himself, emerging from a woman's womb – yet fully God and fully man – dying for our sins and raised to life for our righteousness. These are either miraculous events or lies, but they cannot be both. There is no other basis on which theology can be done rationally.

If the Bible is a collection of myths, then it is disqualified by its own terms of reference because it claims to be true. To throw out the miracles in the Bible is to swim against the tide of biblical evidence about itself and to make Jesus a contradiction in terms. Jesus's attitude was that these very miracles were the validation of his Sonship and the sign that the Kingdom of God had come to earth (Luke 4:14–21; 11:20; John 14:11). In fact this was the very reason why Jesus arrived so late at Lazarus's tomb; the miracle would be evidence of his Sonship and God's power to raise the dead (John 11:42).

The apostles shared Jesus's attitude. God's ability to intervene in the natural world was for them one of the distinguishing features of his presence with them and they saw a clear line of continuity between the things Jesus did and their ability to perform similar acts of wonder. What all the people saw as a miraculous act Peter shrugged off as something God does all the time (Acts 3:12, 16)! Indeed, Peter later described one unusual healing as 'an act of kindness shown to a cripple' (Acts 4:9). This was entirely in line with Jesus's habit of 'doing good and healing all who were under the power of the devil' (Acts 10:38). Perhaps the most notable example of the behaviour of the early Christians in this respect was their prayer under pressure: 'Now, Lord, consider their threats and enable your servants to speak your word with great boldness. Stretch out your hand to heal and perform miraculous signs and wonders through the name of your holy servant Jesus' (Acts 4:29–30).

Paul, who belonged to the second wave of apostles, saw things in exactly the same way. Miracles weren't everything in Paul's work; he did more than anyone else in the first century to help us make sense of our faith. But as far as Paul was concerned, miracles were part and parcel of the gospel of which he was not ashamed: 'My message and my preaching were not with wise and persuasive words, but with a demonstration of the Spirit's power, so that your faith might not rest on human wisdom, but on God's power' (1 Corinthians 2:4–5).

Some people want the Bible without miracles, but the resulting account of God's dealings with humans is simply not credible. It is impossible to tell the story of Jesus without using all of the text of the Gospels and that includes miracles.

The no body case

The earliest apostolic preaching after the resurrection was an intriguing kind of bluff-calling. At every given opportunity the disciples spoke about Jesus's death and resurrection (Acts 2:23–4, 36; 3:15; 4:10; 10:39–40). Usually they were doing it in the presence of the very people who had put about a vicious rumour that the disciples had stolen the body of Jesus (Matthew 28:11–15). It's important to remember that the accusers had not seen that body themselves. All the authorities had to go on was the frantic report the guards brought back that Sunday morning. Apart from the disciples and the five hundred believers who saw Jesus, these guards were the only eyewitnesses to the strange events. As they heard the disciples presenting the incredible story of the resurrection of Jesus with such boldness, the authorities had a limited number of choices. They could own up and join in; they could accuse them of necromancy and order that the disciples give up the body; or they could demand that they shut up. They chose the third option. But even as they confronted the disciples over the issue, they were aware that the disciples knew the truth of the matter. The authorities had pushed themselves into a terrible corner and lost the credibility battle.

So the disciples were calling the authorities' bluff in that they knew Jesus was alive again, they knew they were innocent of stealing the body, and they knew that the authorities knew they hadn't stolen it! Everybody would have realised how improbable it was that a group of Galileans from the north would have broken an official seal on a rich man's tomb. The consequences would have been dire. Also, it was anathema for a Jew to touch a dead body. And in any event everyone knew that just a few days earlier all the disciples had been afraid to be associated with Jesus alive –

let alone dead. And if they really had stolen the body and refused to give it up, why couldn't the authorities use force and obtain it from them, to dispel the resurrection idea?

No group has ever insisted on a resurrection with such consistent passion. The authorities must have seen that any attempt to get the disciples to hand over the body of Jesus would have met not with arguments, refusals or counter claims about what *really* went on outside the tomb, but with renewed proclamation of the resurrection. By all accounts, the disciples were not looking to win arguments, they merely wanted to tell what they had seen (Acts 5:27–8). So they were never asked about the body they were accused of stealing.

John Montgomery summed it up well:

> It passes the bounds of credibility that the early Christians could have manufactured such a tale and then preached it among those who might easily have refuted it simply by producing the body of Jesus.
>
> (quoted by Josh McDowell, *The Resurrection Factor*, Paternoster, 1988)

The opposition had lost its strongest argument; there was, so to speak, no body to support their denials.

Paul wasn't there at the time of the resurrection, but when he met the risen Jesus on his way to persecute Christians (Acts 9) his life was changed forever. It may well have been an existential experience, but that takes nothing away from its historical reality. The intellectual, strait-laced Pharisee was hardly likely to know such a complete transformation based on a one-off, impressive emotion. Paul was not hallucinating on the Damascus Road. God chose a hard-headed rationalist to take the good news to Gentiles and deliberately chose a most unlikely candidate. Such a person would not change so completely as a result of one brief encounter. Paul didn't just experience *something*, he met Someone. This was the same resurrected Lord he went on to pursue for the rest of his life (Philippians 3:10–11). Paul the ex-assassin even suspected that it was his complete conviction about the resurrection which finally lost him his liberty (Acts 23:6).

Would you credit it?

A few weeks after the resurrection Jerusalem was in deep confusion. Everyone was still talking about '*the*' crucifixion. You couldn't avoid it. As the downcast disciples on the Emmaus Road said to the 'stranger', only a visitor would have missed the headlines (Luke 24:18). Within fifty days there were rumours flying around. One was the official version that Jesus's body had been taken away mysteriously by his disciples. Then there was a second rumour being put about that he had been resurrected. People just weren't sure about the first claim; it wasn't adding up because no one had been charged with breaking the official seal on the tomb. Presumably the job of identifying the culprits wouldn't have been all *that* difficult, because trained soldiers would have been able to identify who had done it. In any case, the people most likely to have done it were a very conspicuous and vocal group from the north who were going around telling everyone that this Jesus was still alive! More than that, they were claiming that he was the Messiah. The only problem with their story was that they were the only ones who claimed to have seen him after he came back to life. The unofficial report said that about five hundred had seen him. But that was difficult too, because the people who saw him over a forty-day period were all his followers. It would have been much more convincing had Jesus showed up outside the High Priest's front door or paid a return visit to Pilate or Herod. He could even have looked up the soldiers who crucified him. He kept it strictly to his followers – which all sounded suspiciously 'in-crowd'. Even the convincing proof Jesus offered to the sceptical Thomas had taken place entirely behind closed doors (John 20:26–8).

But within twelve months of these strange events, Jerusalem had been completely transformed. The story had spread so far and was attracting so many followers that the authorities had no idea what to do – apart from using force to try and stop it. Within a short period of time, the whole thing had gone past arguments and, in any case, it was becoming quite clear that the new group had more credibility with the people.

Whenever the two groups met they saw things from very different points of view. The one had vested interests in disbelieving the things they heard and the other had a historical, life-transforming experience they could not deny.

Faith, reason and the resurrection

Not much has changed since then. But over the past fifty years, Christians who refuse to deny miracles have been working much harder to show 'proofs' for resurrection. Among the host of materials available, people like C.S. Lewis have done a great deal to help develop a rational approach to the Gospels that brings faith and reason together. Anyone who has read Frank Morrison's *Who Moved the Stone?* (Zondervan) will find there a good deal of compelling evidence for the historical reliability of the resurrection. Morrison set out to disprove the biblical claims of the resurrection and ended up as a believer. His chapter, 'The book that refused to be written', gives an account of his journey to faith. Similarly, populist Josh McDowell has spent over thirty years as an apologist for the resurrection. His two foremost works, *Evidence that Demands a Verdict* (Vida Publishing, 1982) and *The Resurrection Factor* have been used widely over the years. In the first of the two books, McDowell identified over 14,000 documents proving the historical reliability of the Bible. In his second book, he confidently estimated 24,633 proofs for the Bible as a historically reliable document.

The difficulty with the best arguments Christians offer is that they are always likely to rely on circular proof. The Bible certainly believes in the resurrection: it is mentioned over one hundred times in the New Testament. As an intellectual exercise, the biblical evidence for the resurrection is coherent and persuasive – if you believe the Bible. That is why proof of the resurrection will always be bound up with the historical reliability of the Bible itself. But the resurrection is not scientifically *conclusive* in the same way that the law of gravity is. Conclusive proof for the resurrection would be the same physical Jesus with nail prints appearing in Jerusalem every Easter since AD 33. Jesus chose not to do that. He did not even show himself to anyone outside the community of believers. This is a challenge to faith.

The resurrection as a historical fact will always provoke problems but it is still an integral part of the good news. For those of us who have met the Risen Christ, faith has agreed with the data of the Bible and the corroborating evidence of the biblical accounts from other sources in the early years. Faith and reason have always had a place together around the empty tomb of Jesus. This was why Paul could talk to Festus about his faith, which was 'true and reasonable' (Acts 26:25).

But in the same way that the fact of the resurrection powerfully reached across from the believing community of five hundred to turn the world upside down, so the story keeps spilling over the edges of the Christian community to others for whom it is credible and believable. In March 1998 Melvyn Bragg, the writer and broadcaster, was interviewed by the *War Cry* on his views on the resurrection. Bragg, who described himself at the end of the interview as someone 'still struggling' with faith, said,

The resurrection is the crucial question in Christianity. It is where the act of faith comes in. The rest you can talk about as myth. You can talk about the myth of the virgin birth. You can talk about the ascension as myth. But the resurrection of Jesus is the crucial question. Because if he was raised to life, Jesus Christ is the Son of God.

Spreading the rumour

There were good reasons why the resurrection rumour won the day. For one thing, the disciples themselves had changed. They emerged from the upper room with a new confidence in the message. Even the authorities noticed that something dramatic had happened to these people; they had been with Jesus (Acts 4:13). In the simplest marketing terms we all know that confidence in a product makes an awful lot of difference to the sales figures. The rumour of the resurrection spread because the disciples believed it and spoke about it with great confidence. They took every opportunity to tell people about it, and even when there was good reason to retreat into a defensive position they presented a positive approach to their faith.

It is a kind of confidence which is seldom seen among us today. We have a tendency to be apologetic about our faith, to obscure it for as long as our conscience will allow us. In an environment which pushes us easily into defence mode, many of us have to be flushed out by other people's curiosity or powers of deduction rather than owning up to our relationship with the Lord of the resurrection. It is much easier to hide behind the idea that 'people don't want religion stuffed down their throats'. That is often true, and many of us can cite embarrassing examples of inappropriate harassment done in the name of Christian love. However, many of us also know that we have walked away from open opportunities to talk sensitively about Jesus with enthusiasm. Enthusiasm is infectious. People are likely to be drawn to it even before they have given us a full hearing.

As well as being confident, the first Christians were also positive. There were no signs of self-pity with the disciples. Neither opposition nor persecution seemed to slow them down. Having been flogged and released, they rejoiced, 'because they had been counted worthy of suffering disgrace for the Name' (Acts 5:41).

Their culture was more amenable to the message of resurrection than we may realise at first glance. The idea of life after death was not entirely strange. Jesus found a concept of reincarnation already woven into the fabric of life when he healed the man born blind (John 9). That is the explanation behind the question he faced: 'Who sinned, this man or his parents, that he was born blind?' Presumably, the only way in which he could be responsible for his blindness at birth would be that he had sinned in some previous life. And if Jesus's disciples believed it, it must have been a widespread idea at the time. The Pharisees believed in resurrection. Mary and Martha believed that Lazarus would be raised at the last day (John 11:24).

So the disciples met very little opposition to the *idea* of a resurrection. Even before King Agrippa, Paul argued for the reasonableness of resurrection. 'Why should any of you consider it incredible that God raises the dead?' Paul asked (Acts 26:8). In fact the only negative response Paul had from the nobles he spoke to was when he suggested that Gentiles were accepted by God. That was the point at which Festus accused him of studying too hard (Acts 26:24). It was exactly the response he had received saying the same thing to the Jews when he was arrested in Jerusalem (Acts 26:21).

The society that had to come to terms with the apostles and their testimony to the resurrection of Jesus was a multifaceted one in which different cultures – even within Judaism – sat side by side. Those early years saw ferment at the cultural crossroads created by Roman globalisation. Society was influenced by Greek, Persian, Roman and Jewish civilisations. Jerusalem was a city in which, when Jesus was described as 'King of the Jews', it had to be written in three languages (John 19:20). Diversity was in. Modern cosmopolitan centres are now closer to the New Testament than we may think. Pluralism presents real challenges for Christian truth but it also opens up equally important opportunities.

Some time ago my daughter, then aged thirteen, asked what she regarded as a perfectly ordinary question. 'Dad,' she called out, 'do you believe in UFOs?' I said, 'Not really', and thought how unusual such a question would have been twenty or thirty years earlier. The flood of science fiction influences such as *The X Files*, *Quantum Leap* and *Star Trek* has contributed to the build-up of a generation of adults that is prepared to suspend reason temporarily while living in a very materialistic, real world. My son, who is an otherwise rational person, becomes deeply distressed if he misses an episode of *Star Trek*. Today, as we have noted before, 65 per cent of adults in Britain believe in the paranormal.

In 1990 a Gallup poll of religious belief in Europe showed that 66 per cent of people believe we have souls and 52 per cent believe in life after death. Interestingly, a 1997 European Youth Survey showed 58 per cent of young people who did not believe in God still believed in life after death, and 57 per cent were convinced of the existence of ghosts. When the Easter Enigma conducted a nationwide survey in April 1996, they found that half the respondents believed that it was necessary to believe in the resurrection in order to be a Christian.

While increasing numbers of people no longer have any real confidence in church – or church leaders – people are showing increasing signs of spiritual sensitivity together with a willingness to believe the unbelievable. This is why we are faced with an increasing number of cults that believe in such bizarre things as saviours arriving in spacecraft. In this environment, Christians may have less reason to be nervous about the resurrection than we may have thought. The bankruptcy of this secular and materialistic age, together with the rise of New Age thinking and the develop-ment of new scientific frontiers in genetics, for example, are pushing our culture out of its purely rational box to the point where people are willing to think the unthinkable. As we continue to look further into space than we may ever travel we are beginning to think that 'all things are possible'.

The irony is that those Christian leaders who encourage us to leave miracles behind may actually be more out of touch with the culture than those of us who have the courage to tell the story as we find it in the Bible. The empty tomb was never meant to be an assault on our intelligence; it harmonises faith and reason. When we have met with the Risen Christ, we, like Paul, will still have to contend with many people who will ridicule and sneer in disbelief, but more others may want to hear us on this than we might believe (Acts 17:32).

Proud to proclaim

Our Christian witness need not be complex or unapproachable. Christian faith has preserved at its centre three enduring symbols – the cradle, the cross and the empty tomb – which have become inseparable from its message and with which all of us can identify at some point in our lives. Each Christmas as our family and friends are caught up in the commercialised celebrations and festivities, people will still recognise the simplicity and wonder of the idea of the baby in the cradle. It is our opportunity to remind them and ourselves that God is never far from our weaknesses and vulnerabilities. God is not limited to big names or strong people.

But we also have a passionate God who expressed his passion in the supreme death of his Son on the cross. And whatever we may or may not understand about the details of this death so long ago, we are not allowed to escape its compelling message: God is not afraid of our sins or our suffering. Even if the twenty-first century does all it can to sanitise the problem of human pain, God is willing to stand in it with us.

The good news is that God not only stands with us; through the resurrection he is able to offer hope in and beyond our suffering. When we have the courage to take the empty tomb seriously, we share in the quality of life beyond the grave which Jesus himself demonstrated on Easter Sunday.

This is indeed a gospel of which we need not be ashamed, that we can be proud to proclaim.

Also by Joel Edwards

Lord, Make Us One
– But Not All the Same!

Seeking Unity in Diversity

How is it possible that a black Pentecostal could find himself at the heart of British evangelicalism? Joel Edwards tells the story of his own pilgrimage from the close-knit black church community in Britain to his role as General Director of the Evangelical Alliance, where he holds in tension a variety of different viewpoints.

As a young Christian Joel belonged to a church which enjoyed powerful teaching and exuberant Pentecostal worship but where jewellery was frowned on. Joel describes how he was plunged into the melting-pot of London Bible College where he encountered students from very different cultural and church backgrounds. He compares his experience with the challenge to find unity in diversity which faces evangelicals today. He urges both greater understanding and the importance of putting private prejudices aside in favour of faithfulness to non-negotiable truths.

Published by Hodder & Stoughton
ISBN 0 340 72171 5